THE ADEQUATE MAN

PAUL S. REES

The Adequate Man

PAUL IN PHILIPPIANS

FLEMING H. REVELL COMPANY

Westwood, New Jersey
London E.C.4—29 Ludgate Hill
Glasgow C.2—229 Bothwell Street

Library of Congress Catalog Card Number: 59-8720

Printed in the United States of America

To

DAN

AN ONLY SON
WHOSE ARENA FOR CHRISTIAN
WITNESS IS NOT A PULPIT BUT AN
OFFICE

One of our distinguished American ministers is Dr. Daniel Poling, editor of the American *Christian Herald* and for many years President of Christian Endeavour International. Dr. Poling, as some of you may know, had a preacher son who was one of the four chaplains who went down on the *Dorchester* not far from your British coast, in those dark days of World War II. They gave their life-belts to the fellows, these four chaplains who went down with the ship. Now Clark Poling was not only the son of a distinguished minister, but he was the father of a lovely family, and before he left he wrote a letter to the family and to his father and mother; and in that letter he said, "I know I shall have your prayers; but please don't pray simply that God will keep me safe. War is a dangerous business. Pray that God will make me adequate."

FOREWORD

It is hoped that what follows may turn out to be more than an essay in exposition. It seems to me that a service sometimes overlooked is that of making Holy Scripture not only more *understandable* but more *lovable.* The *light* we must have; if, in addition, we can have the *lure,* so much the better.

It will be found that the treatment of *Philippians* herein presented is author-centred rather than text-centred. The epistle is in fact a remarkable self-portrait of the apostle who wrote it.

So to the hope already expressed may be added another: that St. Paul himself, a man not always easy to understand and sometimes regarded as an enigmatic and unattractive personality, will be seen far more as a human friend to be appreciated and less as a problematical figure to be analysed.

The Revised Standard Version has been used as the basic text for our exposition. Whatever its weaknesses as a translation—and it has them—this version renders the Pauline writings, especially the more difficult passages, with extraordinary lucidity and accuracy. Permission to quote from it, under copyrights of 1946 and 1952, has been given by the Division of Christian Education of the National Council of Churches.

For the encouragement I have received, along with helpful suggestions, from Mr. Arthur Chapple, I must here record my thanks. Indeed, he must be credited with having given the book its title.

My secretary, Miss Georgia Ryan, has been at once patient and painstaking in handling the numerous details of preparing the manuscript. I shall always be grateful for the wedding of skill and good cheer that I witnessed in her.

To whom else am I indebted? Ah, my soul, that is the question that is shatteringly humbling! To countless benefactors, known and unknown!

But chiefly:

"To God the Father, God the Son,
And Spirit we adore;
All praise and honour, glory, power,
Be now and evermore."

Minneapolis, Minnesota — PAUL S. REES.

CONTENTS

I

THE ART OF THE HEART

I

THE ART OF THE HEART

FOR what may a city of the remote past be remembered?

For a variety of things, obviously.

For continuity across the centuries: such is *Rome's* distinction.

For architectural glory and lavish elegance: such was *Babylon's* bid for "immortality."

For cultural brilliance: such was *Athens'* claim upon the world's remembrance.

For a distinctive quality in its citizens: such is the persistent fame of *Sparta*.

For an extraordinary tradition of religious faith and devotion: such is the deathless repute in which *Jerusalem* is held.

But in ancient Macedonia, not far from the western shoreline of the Aegean Sea, once stood a city that lives on in human memory for none of these reasons. To be sure, its nearby deposits of silver and gold once yielded fabulous wealth, but the mines were long ago exhausted. To be sure, Philip II, father of Alexander the Great, made it a fortified town and bestowed on it his own name. To be sure, it became, in 42 B.C., the site of the famous battle in which the forces of Octavian and Mark Antony defeated those of Brutus and Cassius, with Octavian subsequently assuming the title of "Caesar Augustus." To be sure, the city was given the status of a Roman "colony," and the pretentious title of "Colonia August Julia Philippensis."

These honours, such as they were, have long since faded, and with them the city's very existence. What remains today is an assortment of melancholy ruins, chief among which are those of a temple built to the honour of the Roman god Silvanus.

Thus passed "the boast of heraldry" and "the pomp of power" that once belonged to this privileged metropolis of Macedonia.

What then accounts for the fact that every week in the year there are millions of human beings who see in print or hear in speech a word that perpetuates Philippi's memory?

The astonishing reply is that, sometime in A.D. 61 or 62, a Christian prisoner named Paul wrote a letter to some Christian friends of his at Philippi. That did it!

In the ordering of God, as we Christians believe, that letter made its way into the collection of holy writings known as the New Testament. In consequence Philippi will have a memorial as long as there is a Bible to read anywhere in the world.

Philippians gives us a Paul whom we do not see, for example, in *Galatians* or *Corinthians*. It is a Paul so winsomely human, writing to friends so humanly dear about matters so disarmingly natural that we wonder if the *theologian* has not been swallowed up in the *friend* and the *apostle* who must defend his authority has not resigned in favour of the *comrade* who must divulge his love and say his thanks.

In light of this, it is perhaps not at all surprising to find that this letter is without logical format. In common with other epistles he wrote, *Philippians* does indeed have a salutation at the beginning and a combination of benediction and salutation at the close. As for its principal contents, they unfold intimately and informally, ranging through such topics as a personal report on the health of one who was held in mutually high regard by Paul and the members of the Philippian congregation, the reasons why another friend would pay them a visit in the near future, the necessity of having a good talk with two of the ladies of the church who were not on the best terms with each other, and the warm gratitude he felt toward his Philippian friends for the gift of money they had sent to him by the hand of one of their members.

Obviously there would be more to the epistle than this, else it would not have found its place among the permanent documents of the New Testament. Woven into this informality are insights and principles that are of first-rate importance to the Christian and to the Christian community. Running through it is a stream of cheerfulness that ripples and sings, and gives to any sensitive reader a feeling of the sheer joy there is in a life which Christ has redeemed and within which He resides through His Spirit. In the Paul who penned *Philippians* one sees both the art and the heart of living, according to the Christian pattern.

Our comment on the customary questions will be brief:

Where was Philippians written? Three places have been discussed by the scholars as possibilities: Ephesus, Caesarea, and Rome. The traditional position that it was Rome seems still to have the best of the argument.

When was it written? Certainty still eludes the historian's quest—probably always will. Fairly beyond doubt is the view that it was composed during the Roman imprisonment, which is often referred to as the "first" imprisonment on the assumption that the apostle was released and subsequently re-arrested before execution. On this view the date of writing would fall within the two-year period of 60–62. Left unresolved is the question of whether *Philippians* was dispatched near the beginning or the end of this period. Manifestly, precision of date has almost nothing to do with the abiding values which the letter holds.

Why was it written? The reasons, superficially, are thoroughly human and mundane. Chief among them was the fact that the members of the Philippian church had made up a gift of money and sent it to Paul by Epaphroditus, one of their members. This timely and valued gift must be acknowledged with thanks. A secondary occasion for writing, which nevertheless turns out to be extraordinarily important, was the report that Epaphroditus evidently brought concerning some friction between two of the members of the congregation. The endangered unity of the church, together with perils to truth created by misleading teachers, called forth some notable passages in which there is either an exquisite sublimity (2: 5–11) or a withering intensity (3: 1–3).

Still another reason for the letter—a reason that Professor Ernest F. Scott places in the front rank—is to ensure Epaphroditus a good reception on his return to the church. He had been sent with the purpose of his remaining with Paul. His illness and homesickness, however, made Paul feel that he should return home. Hence the explanation and the appeal that we find in 2: 25–30.

By whom was it written? Only a small school of radical critics, headed by Baur many years ago, has challenged the Pauline authorship. Baur's attempt has been called by that famous New Testament scholar, Dean Alford, an illustration of "the insanity of hypercriticism."[1] The dogmatism of Simcox appears to be justified: "If this letter was not written by Paul, nothing was."[2]

And how shall we rank this man Paul? Says Deissmann, "The historian, surveying the beginnings of Christianity, sees St. Paul as first after Jesus." Since Jesus was the God-Man, His category

[1] Cf. the "Introduction" to Philippians in the *Philippians-Colossians* volume of "The Pulpit Commentary." New York: Funk and Wagnalls, p. xii.

[2] C. E. Simcox, *They Met At Philippi*. New York: Oxford University Press, p. 21.

is unique. If Paul is "first after Jesus," there is no extravagance in calling him the greatest of humans.

Deissmann goes on to observe that what we care for most is "the living man, Paul, whom we hear speaking and see gesticulating, here playful, gentle as a father, and tenderly coaxing, so as to win the hearts of the infatuated children—there thundering and lightning with the passionate wrath of a Luther, with cutting irony and bitter sarcasm on his lips."[1] One might take exception to the phrase "bitter sarcasm," preferring the word "biting" to "bitter," but the tribute as a whole is worthy.

Professor Henry Drummond once described Dwight L. Moody as "the greatest human I have ever met." It is no reflection on Moody to say that if Professor Drummond had met St. Paul he would have revised his judgment.

It is now proposed that we examine this portrait of Paul, the greatest of humans, in this most human of all his epistles—the letter to the Philippians.

These are the tones to brace and cheer
The lonely watcher of the fold.
When nights are dark, and foemen near,
When visions fade and hearts are cold.

How timely then a comrade's song
Comes floating on the mountain air,
And bids thee yet be bold and strong—
Fancy may die, but Faith is there.

JOHN KEBLE.

[1]Cf. *The International Standard Bible Encyclopedia,* Vol. IV. Grand Rapids: Eerdmans, p. 2277.

II

THE AFFECTIONATE MAN

II

THE AFFECTIONATE MAN

PROFESSOR DAVID SMITH, in his *Life and Letters of St. Paul,* conjectures that the apostle sent this letter to the Philippians in the month of November of the year 60.[1] If so, the chilliness of the season offered a sharp contrast to the warmth and the charm of the message that Epaphroditus carried with him when, recovered from his serious illness, he set off from the Imperial City to return to his home in Philippi. Tucked away under his tunic was the message that David Smith calls the "sweetest and tenderest" thing to be found in all of St. Paul's correspondence.

Without a rich endowment of affection no man could write what we are now to examine in the first section of this letter. "I hold you in my heart," he will say to them in verse 7; and, holding them there, he will let his heart utter itself with gracious and graceful abandon.

SALUTATION

Ancient custom in correspondence called for a more formal opening than we moderns hold necessary. In at least one particular the ancients were better time-savers than we are. Have you not opened a letter, done in typescript or in handwriting that you did not recognize, and, curious to know who in all the land was writing you, you had to look down at the bottom of the page or perhaps turn over the page to find a signature? Look now at the letter before you, and see how far you have to proceed in order to find the signature! Not at the end but at the beginning: "Paul!"

This salutation includes *sender, subjects,* and *substance.* The sender is the apostle, who in the case of the loyal Philippians does not find it necessary to invoke the authority of that title. Joint

[1]Phillips, in his introduction to Philippians in *Letters To Young Churches,* appears to reflect the view of a majority of New Testament scholars when he gives the date as "about 62."

sender (though not joint writer) is his junior companion, Timothy, included in the greeting because of Paul's magnanimous spirit and because Timothy was well known and loved by the Philippian Christians.

The *subjects* are "all the saints in Christ Jesus who are at Philippi." Some would say, "You are a saint if you have been *canonized*," which usually means something that occurs long after you are dead. Some would say, "You are a saint if you have been *cleansed*," such cleansing being understood as complete ethical purgation. But what the New Testament says is, "You are a saint if you have been *claimed*." The "saints" at Philippi, or at Ephesus, or at Rome, are those who, regardless of the stage of spiritual development they may have reached or not reached, belong to Jesus Christ, possess His life, have received His Holy Spirit. To be sure, the word has implications that narrow its meaning—implications which, I dare say, were vividly in the mind of Lacordaire when he cried, "O God, give us some saints!"—but we will need to bow, nevertheless, to the correctness of J. B. Phillips when for "saints" he uses the expression "true Christians."

The salutation out of the way, Paul the affectionate is ready to write of those intimate matters that form a living bond between him and his friends at Philippi.

I

HIS PRAISE

"I thank my God in all my remembrance of you, always in every prayer of mine for you all making my prayer with joy, thankful for your partnership in the gospel from the first day until now. And I am sure that he who began a good work in you will bring it to completion at the day of Jesus Christ. It is right for me to feel thus about you all, because I hold you in my heart, for you are all partakers with me of grace, both in my imprisonment and in the defence and confirmation of the gospel. For God is my witness, how I yearn for you all with the affection of Christ Jesus" (1 : 3–8).

His whole soul is a carillon, and the first bell to be struck is that of thanksgiving. The call to rejoice, as we shall see, is sounded so often in these chapters that many a student has subtitled Philippians "the Epistle of Joy."

For St. Paul there is the *joy of recollection*: "I thank my God in all my remembrance of you" (v. 3). What an inventory of memories he would have! That Sabbath Day when he had met with a small group of Lydia's friends "on the clean bank of the Gangites" and there, while he had told the good news of "Messiah Jesus," as Arthur Way is always putting it, the heart of this influential business woman had been "opened" and she had become the firstfruits of the Gospel in Europe!

Or that morning, in the pre-dawn darkness, when the Philippian jailer, suddenly made new in Christ, gave tender aid to the battered and bleeding backs of Paul and Silas!

Or those previous occasions when out of their slender resources they had scraped together a gift of money and forwarded it to him!

"The man who has forgotten to be thankful," said Robert Louis Stevenson, "has fallen asleep in life." Never was this species of drowsiness permitted to overcome the praiseful prisoner who now, narrowly restricted at Rome, ranges back through the yesterdays to taste the joy of recollection.

There was, moreover, the *joy of intercession*: "always in every prayer of mine for you all making my prayer with joy" (v. 4). One expositor makes this verse the pretext for asking the question: "How many American Christians prayed for Hitler and Mussolini during the war?" It is a fair question, I grant. But it is not so easy to grant that it should be raised by way of interpreting or applying *this* lovely word in verse 4. Any prayer for those sinister souls, with their egos running wild, must have been a prayer of grief, a prayer of deep and distressful longing for their redemption. Totally different in mood and outlook was this gladsome intercession that Paul carried forward in behalf of his valued comrades in Christ. For some, Paul prayed with pain; for these, with pleasure.

And there was the *joy of participation*: "thankful for your partnership in the gospel from the first day until now" (v. 5). The word for "partnership" is *koinonia*. The reader of the New Testament comes upon it again and again. It is full of force and flavour. Professor E. F. Scott holds that three distinguishable strands of meaning are woven into it: (1) the fellowship of Christians with one another; (2) the communion of Christians with Christ or the Holy Spirit; and (3) the sharing of possessions.

There is no reason why we should exclude any of these meanings from the word as it is here used by the apostle. A smaller soul than Paul's would never have spoken so humbly, so *inter-*

dependently. If they had needed him, he had needed them; and interlaced with both needs was their common need of Christ. This, to borrow a phrase that one author applies to Abraham Lincoln, is "craftsmanship in the art of human relations."

Again, there is the *joy of anticipation*: "And I am sure that he who began a good work in you will bring it to completion at the day of Jesus" (v. 6). One wishes that such a sentence as this could be allowed to speak its own assuring message without having to be run through the matrix of some rigid theological presupposition that happens to be ours. The Bible is a book of extremes and yet it is a book of balance. St. Paul was capable of strong, even of vehement, utterances, but if you follow him to the end, you will find his balance—always.

Later in this letter the apostle will regard it as no contradiction of the confidence here expressed when he urges these believers to hold "fast the word of life" lest it be shown that he, their spiritual father, did "run in vain or labour in vain" (2: 16).

'I see you,' cries Paul, 'I see you, my brethren, as you will be when our Lord comes again and you are clothed with the likeness of His resurrection. It was neither of your deserving or of your doing that the work of grace was begun in you. It will be neither of your deserving or of your doing that this work will at last be completed. It will be His mercy and His might all the way. God the initiator is also God the finisher!'

Thus, with the joy of recollection, of intercession, of participation, and of anticipation, the apostolic heart flows out in affectionate praise. And if anyone complains that Paul is going to excess, he is ready to demur. "It is right for me to feel thus about you all," he insists, quite deliberately (v. 7). He adds, strongly, that it is with the very "affection of Christ Jesus" that he loves them and longs for them.

And now the soul of this absent pastor turns from song to supplication.

II

HIS PRAYER

"And it is my prayer that your love may abound more and more, with knowledge and all discernment, so that you may approve what is excellent, and may be pure and blameless for the day of Christ, filled with the fruits of righteousness which come through Jesus Christ, to the glory and praise of God" (1: 9–11).

First, there is the *petition* itself: "that your love may abound more and more." Forgive the redundancy, but this is *agape* love. It is not erotic love, nor social love, but filial love: it is *divine* love. It is God's love in Christ through the Holy Spirit. It is this love released and set to work in redeemed men and women. As such, it is reciprocal love: God's saving good-will to us, creating, evoking, a response which says,

"My Jesus, I love Thee,
I know Thou art mine,
For Thee all the follies
Of sin I resign."

And since this is His love in us, it means that we love those whom He loves. Thus Bishop Moule feels, rightly, I suspect, that "your love" in this verse is to be understood "above all in the sense of your love to one another."[1] And this is to be no meagre, shrunken thing, but something ample, abundant, tidal. The Greek word for "abound" signifies a *running over.* Our English word "abound" has of course a Latin ancestry that, when spelled out literally, means "wave upon wave." 'My prayer for you,' says the apostle, 'is that your love for one another will never be doled out in parsimonious pinches, but will rather tumble forth like some magnificent cascade.'

Secondly, such a prayer has an *implication.* It implies that before God's love can overflow us it must be received by us. Before it can abound, it must first abide. For this *agape* is not a natural growth in the garden of unredeemed human nature. It is an exotic. It is a transplantation from God's heart to ours. The *gift* of it must precede the *growth* of it.

The petition is thus for enlargement. The implication is that this enlargement in the Christlike love with which we regard others in the brotherhood of believers is possible only as "God's love has been poured into our hearts through the Holy Spirit which has been given unto us" (Romans 5: 5).

And now follows the *direction* in which the apostle's prayer moves and in which love is to develop: "in spiritual knowledge and in all needed discernment, so that ye may test the things that differ" (v. 9). I have here followed the translation of Bishop Moule.

If we are to be Pauline Christians, it must be clear to us that

[1]H. C. G. Moule, *Philippian Studies.* London: Hodder and Stoughton, p. 28.

there is no rift between the enkindled heart and the enlightened mind. Light without love can be as forbiddingly cold as an iceberg in moonlight. Love without light, on the other hand, can be as flamingly destructive as a forest fire in the dry season.

Associated with Luther and Melanchthon in the fiery struggle of the Reformation were Carlstadt and Munzer. Why are their names almost unknown to us today? Why did their contribution to the cause fizzle out like a Roman candle? Well, as Manschreck points out in his biography of Melanchthon, both men wanted to abolish education, both insisted that the Gospel is for the simple rather than the learned, both encouraged students to leave their books and take up the tools of trade and farming. Munzer, more extreme than Carlstadt, insisted that he had a "living Word" from God that was superior to the written word of Scripture and that he had a divine commission to "inaugurate the kingdom of God by force."[1]

God could have used their warm-heartedness, but He had severely to discount their hot-headedness. Love as unregulated impulse is dangerous. Love giving itself to hard thinking and sensitive discrimination is a delight to God and a priceless benediction to the Church and society.

How, otherwise, shall we "approve what is excellent," as this prayer beautifully puts it in verse 10? "To put to the proof the things that differ," may be a more exact translation (though this is disputed by some scholars), but it brings us out at the same turning, it seems to me. For when the Christian thinks his way, under love's piloting, to decisions between what is "right" and "wrong," or "good" and "better," is it not for the purpose of "approving what is excellent"?

Most of us tend to forget that New Testament Christianity has a place both for absolutes and for relativities. Confusion arises when we fail to see the difference between an absolute—the absolute prohibition, let us say, of idolatry—and a relativity, such as, let us say, the principle of being thankful. Jesus once healed a leper. Mark tells us that the Master told him to keep quiet about it: "See thou say nothing to any man" (Mark 1:44). But the man was thrilled over his deliverance—and as thankful as thrilled. Ignoring the Master's instruction, he "went out," says Mark, "and began to publish it much, and to blaze abroad the matter, insomuch that Jesus could no more openly enter into the city" (v. 45).

[1]C. Manschreck, *Melanchthon: The Quiet Reformer*. Nashville: Abingdon, 1958, p. 123.

Now, is it not good to give thanks? In principle, yes. But what the leper's case indicates is that conduct may be good in principle without being right in the situation. His love and gratitude were shortsighted: he failed to see that, in that situation and at that stage of Jesus' ministry, he was doing more harm than good. Good as thanksgiving is, the "excellent" thing *for this man* and *at that time* would have been the obedience of silence.

Similar complexities face all of us almost every day. Take, for example, the Christian concept of modesty, especially (though not exclusively) as it applies to the appearance and conduct of our girls and women. The Quaker home into which I was born, and for which I cherish an imperishable gratitude, combined in some ways the stern traditions of the Spartans and the Puritans. My mother, for example, both bore me and reared me without ever wearing a wedding ring. For the wedding band was put in the category of needless jewellery and therefore of immodest self-display.

But when I was a quarter of a century old and accompanied my parents on a trip abroad, my mother had on her finger the ringed symbol of her wedded life. Why? Had modesty and simplicity ceased to be good in principle? Not at all. All that had ceased was the rightness of her particular sign of this modesty. She was now about to move among peoples—including the "saints"—in other parts of the world where in fact *not* to have on the ring would be interpreted as something decidedly immodest. Love's knowledge, love's discernment, gave her to see that in the situation this was the "excellent" thing.

A word of caution is in order here. Since Christians are in varying stages of the life in love, with corresponding differences in their knowledge and insight, allowance must be made for deviations in practice. Here let each of us be as charitable towards others as we are stern with ourselves. Only so shall we be "pure and blameless for the day of Christ, filled with the fruits of righteousness which come through Jesus Christ, to the glory and praise of God" (vs. 10, 11).

Charles Wesley has some lines which, I grant, can be read too narrowly, too much as though all of life's decisions were between obvious black and obvious white, but which, when read understandingly, are a worthy prayer for any of us:

"I want the witness, Lord,
That all I do is right,
According to Thy will and Word,
Well pleasing in Thy sight.

I ask no higher state;
Indulge me but in this,
And soon or later then translate
To my eternal bliss."

III

HIS POISE

"I want you to know, brethren, that what has happened to me has really served to advance the gospel, so that it has become known throughout the whole praetorian guard and to all the rest that my imprisonment is for Christ; and most of the brethren have been made confident in the Lord because of my imprisonment, and are much more bold to speak the word of God without fear.

"Some indeed preach Christ from envy and rivalry, but others from good will. The latter do it out of love, knowing that I am put here for the defence of the gospel; the former proclaim Christ out of partisanship, not sincerely but thinking to afflict me in my imprisonment. What then? Only that in every way, whether in pretence or in truth, Christ is proclaimed; and in that I rejoice.

"Yes, and I shall rejoice. For I know that through your prayers and the help of the Spirit of Jesus Christ this will turn out for my deliverance, as it is my eager expectation and hope that I shall not be at all ashamed, but that with full courage now as always Christ will be honoured in my body, whether by life or by death. For to me to live is Christ, and to die is gain" (1: 12–21).

Far away in Philippi the Christians, knowing that their leader has been made a prisoner by Caesar, are wondering how he fares. Their concern is deep. Their eagerness to know the facts is keen. Their disturbance of mind by reason of contradictory reports about him is a heavy weight. Knowing this, the apostle will set their minds at rest.

When you physically fetter a spirit as daring and venturesome as Paul's, what happens? Do you break it? You do if it is breakable. When you fasten him to a picked member of the Palace Guard, and change that solitary sentinel every six hours of the day and the night, what happens to his dream of preaching more sermons and founding more churches? Do you shatter it? You do if it is shatterable. When you aggravate his trial by the dubious industriousness of those who, out of jealousy and rivalry and the infection of error, assert their leadership in preaching the Gospel and teaching the people, what happens to the calmness of his temper, the magnanimity of his soul? Do you end it then and there? You do if it is endable.

Behold now the magnificent poise that Christ gives this man who is neither frazzled nor finished by all that he is undergoing! 'Really,' he writes, 'you need not worry about me, because "what has happened to me" has "served to advance the gospel" (v. 12). My difficulties have become doors and my thwartings turned into thoroughfares.'

The *character* of this poise may be seen if we sum it up in two sentences: (1) I am in nothing daunted so long as the Gospel is promoted, and (2) I am in nothing daunted so long as Christ is proclaimed.

"To advance the gospel"—that is paramount. Actually, that is what is taking place among these ten thousand soldiers who form the Imperial Guard. When they, and others as well, learn that I am here not for criminal or political reasons but on account of my faith in Christ, their curiosity gives me many a chance to tell the good news. Thus it has become "known throughout the whole praetorian guard . . . that my imprisonment is for Christ" (v. 13). "To advance the gospel"—that is everything. To be chained to a guardsman—that, by comparison, is nothing.

But, after all, these are "the slings and arrows of outrageous fortune" sent Paul's way by non-Christians. An even severer test of our poise arises when fellow Christians take advantage of us or inflict wounds upon us. From this pain Paul did not escape. After gratefully acknowledging that some of "the brethren" were inspired by his example to take loftier ground and hold it with firmer feet, he is obliged to report that there are "others who preach Christ from envy and rivalry" (v. 15). Have it, if you will, that these are "Judaizing Christians" who falsely teach that *grace* and *law* must mingle to make a sinner acceptable to God. I doubt it, though the doubt seems daring in view of the authorities that can be quoted to sustain the view. Or, have it, as I prefer to think, with Vincent and others, that these were indeed Pauline Christians, but men who nevertheless were jealous of Paul. Theirs was a shabbily low state of sanctification in which they were not above using his plight to improve their prestige.

In any case, his word on the situation makes it noon-clear that their inferior motives for preaching Christ will not be allowed to dismay, demoralize or defeat him. Paul's spirit is still on top. Its equilibrium in God is invincible.

'Even though they hope,' says he, '"to make my chains even more galling than they would otherwise be" (v. 17, Phillips), still I find reason to give thanks.' So he goes on, as rendered by Phillips: "However they may look at it, the fact remains that Christ *is* being preached, whether sincerely or not, and that fact makes me very happy" (v. 18).

Ah, my soul, here is the real thing! Here is God's affectionate man so in love with Christ and with Christ's Church that love's anchors hold him no matter how black or beastly the storm!

But now, since anchors have been mentioned, what are they? Poise of this character must have some underlying *confidence* that is not of this world. Since Paul is no man to hide his shining secret, out it comes: "For I know that through your prayers and the help of the Spirit of Jesus Christ this will turn out for my deliverance" (v. 19). Thus the apostle's confidence is (1) in *the prayers of the saints* and (2) in *the power of the Spirit.*

Let me reserve comment on these two matters long enough to clear away some debatable points in the translation and interpretation of certain expressions in this verse. By "clear away" I do not mean that I shall solve the difficulties, which is far beyond my competence. I mean only that I shall take a position. Where the masters disagree, the novices are free—at least within limits!

When the apostle says, "This shall turn to my salvation," I take the word "this" to mean, as Lightfoot holds, "this state of things, these perplexities and annoyances."[1]

In the phrase "the help of the Spirit of Jesus Christ" I take the word "help" to be a feeble translation in the Revised Standard Version, much preferring "the resources of the Spirit" in Phillips, or the "bountiful supply of the Spirit" in Williams, or the "full supply of the Spirit" in Bishop Moule.

The word "salvation"—"this shall turn to my salvation"—I take to mean something other than "deliverance," as in the R.S.V., where obviously the translators understand St. Paul to be speaking of his release from imprisonment. I suggest that it refers to that aspect of the saving process in which the Christian is tested for endurance and proven in service. It is part (though by no means all) of what Paul means when, later in this letter, he will

[1]J. B. Lightfoot, *St. Paul's Epistle To The Philippians*, "Reprint Classic" by Zondervan, Grand Rapids, p. 91.

say, "Work out your own salvation" (2: 12). This interpretation, it seems to me, gathers support from what follows in verse 20: "it is my eager expectation and hope that I shall not be at all ashamed, but that with full courage now as always Christ shall be honoured in my body, whether by life or by death." In fetters or freedom, in dignity or ignominy, in living or dying—what matters? Really nothing, if only the sheer greatness, the unutterable bigness, of Jesus Christ somehow breaks through and becomes luminous in this frail physical frame.

And now back to this twofold confidence that undergirds this triumphant testimony: the confidence that his friends are praying for him and the confidence that the same Holy Spirit whom Jesus possessed in the days of His flesh and whom He bestows from His throne-seat in the Glory will unceasingly empower him.

I doubt that a man ever breathed who believed more ardently in intercessory prayer—the prayer of one for another—than this man Paul. He believed in it as one who *practised* it in love's concern for others and he believed in it as one who *profited* by it in the concern of others for him. If you and I believed in it more, we should make more of it than we do; and so the Church of our praying Saviour would become, to a greater degree than it is, an interlacing network of prayer and power.

"I cannot tell why there should come to me
A thought of someone miles and miles away,
In swift insistence on the memory,
Unless there be a need that I should pray.

Perhaps, just then, my friend has fiercer fight,
A more appalling weakness, a decay
Of courage, darkness, some lost sense of right;
And so, in case he needs my prayer, I pray."

The other root of St. Paul's confidence, by which his unbreakable poise is sustained, is the ministry of the Holy Spirit. "The supply of the Spirit of Jesus Christ," is the excellent rendering of the Authorized Version. The Greek word for "supply" was employed to describe the beneficence of a wealthy citizen who, giving a banquet, would furnish not only the food but a choir of singers to make the evening's delight complete. Hence Professor E. F. Scott says we may translate Paul's words as "a rich provision of the Spirit of Jesus Christ."[1]

[1]E. F. Scott, *The Interpreter's Bible,* Vol. XI. Nashville: Abingdon, p. 34.

If the question be asked, "Is the Holy Spirit Himself the 'supply,' or is the Holy Spirit, who is given by the Father through the Son, the One in whose fullness we find all our needs met with overflowing abundance?" the answer is that either interpretation is allowable. Both are within the New Testament facts.

"A rich provision of the Spirit!" St. Paul experienced it. The question is: Do you and I experience it?

There was that night of which Dr. F. B. Meyer tells, when he walked among the Cumberland hills in solitude, with this prayer on his lips:

"My Father, if there is one soul more than another within the circle of these hills who needs the gift of Pentecost, it is I: I want the Holy Spirit, but I do not know how to receive Him; and I am too weary to think, or feel, or pray intensely."

At which, says Dr. Meyer, an inner Voice spoke: "As you took forgiveness from the hand of the dying Christ, take the Holy Ghost from the hand of the living Christ, and reckon that the gift is thine by a faith that is utterly indifferent to the presence or absence of resultant joy. According to thy *faith,* so shall it be unto thee."

To this the response of his soul was:

"'Lord, as I breathe in this whiff of warm night air, so I breathe into every part of me Thy blessed Spirit.' I felt no hand laid on my head, there was no lambent flame, there was no rushing sound from heaven: but by *faith,* without emotion, without excitement, I took, and took for the first time, and I have kept on taking ever since."[1]

The secret of poise, let us rejoice to say, is not confined to a first-century Paul. It is for Christians of every century. In the ampleness of God's provision there is "an abundant supply of the Spirit," which, combining with the faithful prayers of our Christian comrades, gives us the fortitude that will not collapse under life's pressures or panic in life's emergencies. So far from collapsing, it will confidently hold that "to live is Christ, and to die is gain" (v. 21).

And this confidence, as Maclaren reminds us, is the "true anaesthetic which will give us a 'solemn scorn of ills' and make even the last and greatest change from life to death of little account."[2]

[1]W. Y. Fullerton, *F. B. Meyer, A Biography*. London: Marshall, Morgan & Scott, pp. 65, 66.

[2]A. Maclaren, *Expositions of Holy Scripture,* Vol. 14. Grand Rapids: Eerdmans Publishing Co., p. 218.

IV

HIS PROBLEM

"If it is to be life in the flesh, that means fruitful labour for me. Yet which I shall choose I cannot tell. I am hard pressed between the two. My desire is to depart and be with Christ, for that is far better. But to remain in the flesh is more necessary on your account. Convinced of this, I know that I shall remain and continue with you all, for your progress and joy in the faith, so that in me you may have ample cause to glory in Christ Jesus, because of my coming to you again" (1 : 22–26).

First, let us have the problem *stated*: "My desire is to depart and be with Christ . . . But to remain in the flesh is more necessary on your account" (vs. 23, 24). Hence we have the apostle saying, as translated by Weymouth and Moffatt, "I am in a dilemma." This dilemma is created by the equal pull of *desire* on the one hand and *duty* on the other.

Is the problem *always* so acute with us as to be a dilemma? I think not. If as a young Christian I stand in the morning of my life, I have "the desire" *eventually* to "depart and be with Christ." Meanwhile, however, the call of duty, all urgent and exhilarating, is upon me, and I want to remain for "fruitful labour."

Let it not be forgotten that what led St. Paul to elaborate on this emotional tension between desire and duty was his declaration in verse 21, "For me to live is Christ, and to die is gain." And let it not be forgotten that preachers have taken huge liberties with this sentence, making it say innumerable things which, however true and glorious, were not necessarily in the apostle's thinking when he spoke thus. When read faithfully, in context, its meaning is quite simple. It refers to the practical life of helpfulness, of which Christ is the sum and substance. It refers likewise to the alluring fact that the serving disciple, who has had an ever-growing communion with Christ while alive, will have an even richer communion when death has shifted the scene, without altering the continuity, of his service.

'This being true,' says Paul, 'I find that, at my age and in my circumstances, I front a real dilemma. I am keen to "depart," to be "unloosed," like a ship straining its hawsers, so eager is it for the "bounding main" and the distant port. Still, there is my love for you. There is my longing for more of "the fruit of work" (so Moule) among you. There is my feeling that I am needed by you and others. The surge of desire? Yes. But I must keep a careful eye on it because it is so *self*-regarding. The sense of duty? Yes. And I must give due heed to it because it is *others*-regarding.'

The problem having been clearly stated, let us now see it *solved*: "To remain in the flesh is more necessary on your account. Convinced of this, I know that I shall remain and continue with you all, for your progress and joy in the faith" (vs. 24, 25). The solution is obvious: desire as related to myself subordinated to duty as related to others! A man need have but one eye, and it half-closed, to see how far removed is this view of the future life from the lying caricature fashioned by Communists and others who insist that Christians are a piously selfish lot forever enamoured of "pie in the sky when you die by and by!"

Let Adoniram Judson, Christ's gallant courier to Burma, be a modern witness. Fourteen years have passed since he came out from Massachusetts to this inhospitable land. What does he have to show? For one thing, the graves of his wife and all his children! For another thing, imprisonments so foul and diseases so wasting that he once exclaimed: "If I had not felt certain that every additional trial was ordered by infinite love and mercy, I could not have survived my accumulated sufferings!" Is he ready to call it "quits" and go home to God? Far from it! At this very stage of his painful career, as Boreham has described it, Judson "prayed that he might live to translate the entire Bible into the native language, and to preside over a native church of at least one hundred members."[1]

• So Judson re-incarnates the spirit of Paul. The problem—to live or die, to go or stay—is of course in God's hands; but, insofar as it is ours to express the dedicated mind, we put the good that may come to others by our living above the gain that would come to us by our dying.

Could any solution come closer to the Cross than that?

V

HIS PLEA

"Only let your manner of life be worthy of the gospel of Christ, so that whether I come and see you or am absent, I may hear of you that you stand firm in one spirit, with one

[1] F. W. Boreham, *A Temple of Topaz*. Nashville: Abingdon, p. 139.

mind striving side by side for the faith of the gospel, and not frightened in anything by your opponents. This is a clear omen to them of their destruction, but of your salvation, and that from God. For it has been granted to you that for the sake of Christ you should not only believe in him but also suffer for his sake, engaged in the same conflict which you saw and now hear to be mine" (1 : 27–30).

The affectionate man has now launched well into his tender letter to his friends in Philippi. He has allowed us to gaze into his soul as by an X-ray. We have listened to his praise, with love's ring in it. We have heard his prayer, with love's longing in it. We have marked his poise, with love's serenity in it. We have sympathized with his problem, with love's solution crowning it.

And now the ardour of his love is winsome with wooing.

He pleads for *consistency*: "only let your manner of life be worthy of the gospel of Christ" (v. 27). "Your manner of life," if literally rendered, becomes "your citizen-life." Similarly, the word "worthy" might be given as "weighty."

What sense does this make? Not much, until you remember that Philippi was a Roman colony, with its citizens enjoying the same status, the same prestige, as if they lived in Rome; and until you remember, further, that St. Paul makes use of this situation to light up the truth that these Christians in Philippi are in fact "a colony of heaven." The phrase is Moffatt's. "We are a colony of heaven" is his well-known translation in chapter 3, verse 20.

Now the apostle's plea for consistency begins to make excellent sense. He is saying: 'You profess to be citizens of Christ's commonwealth. Very well, then let the way you live be as weighty as the strong words with which you make this high profession.'

I once sat at the dinner table in Delhi, India, when my host, a churchman with a long record of distinguished service in that land (and a fellow-citizen of the United States), said to me: "You may not have been told that in parts of India, including the great province of Bengal, the traffic in drink is illegal. It is therefore perplexing to many Hindus, and damaging to our American reputation, for drinking parties to be given at the American embassy."

What he was saying, if cast in other language, was this: Americans at the embassy in India, representing a nominally

Christian nation, are adding nothing to the weight or worth of the name "Christian" when indulgence and intoxication seem so important in their lives.

This sets us on the road of Paul's thought. Wherever Christians are, they are the commonwealth of heaven in the framework of earth. Not merely by the things from which they refrain, but by the high things to which they are committed, they are to confirm, and not to contradict, the Gospel.

But note, please, how the plea for consistency is followed by the plea for *constancy*: "stand firm in one spirit, with one mind striving side by side for the faith of the gospel" (v. 27). Here I shall let Vincent and Moffatt and Weymouth go, in favour of Moule and Weiss and Maclaren, and hold that the word "spirit" refers to the Holy Spirit of God. In *Him* we are to find the strength of steadfastness. In *Him* we are to discover the secret of unity. In *Him* we have the sense of unfractured brotherhood.

This constancy, Paul would have us see, must be maintained in two ways:

1. It must be maintained *in the face of persecution*. So firmly are you to stand that you are "not frightened in anything by your opponents" (v. 28). I have somewhere read of a young Hindu who, because he became a Christian, was bitterly censured by his family. When he refused to renounce Christ, he was legally cut off from his share in the large family fortune. Later the brothers and sisters fell to quarrelling over the distribution of his share in the estate. They finally came to him and asked him if he would arbitrate their differences, their reason for asking him being, they said, that he was the only one that all of them would trust.

Isn't that a delicious story? And doesn't it throw at least a little light on this obscure statement by Paul that the courage of the Christians may serve as "a clear omen to them (their opponents) of their destruction, but of your salvation"? (v. 28). Blind to the beauty their brother had seen in Jesus, these relatives nevertheless realized the sheer futility of putting trust in their own collective selfishness, and consequently chose him, their disowned kinsman, as their referee.

2. And then this Christian constancy must be maintained *in the fellowship of pain*: "For it has been granted to you that for the sake of Christ you should not only believe in him but also suffer for his sake."

The word "granted," or "given," as it is in the Authorized Version, has its roots in *charis,* the word for *grace*. 'Out of the

grace of God,' says Paul, 'come these two things as ou
the *trust* by which we take Him as our very own Savi
testing by which we let Him season us in the school o

Consider! In 1946 John Leonard Wilson, Bishop of
not long out of his ghastly war-time internment, s
London over the B.B.C. Said he: "I speak to you th
from personal experience of God's comfort and stren
interned by the Japanese . . . I suffered many hours c
and tortures. Throughout that time I never turned
vain. God was revealed to me, not because I was a spec
but because I was willing *in faith to accept what Go*
know that whether you are despondent or in joy, wh
are apathetic or full of enthusiasm, there is available f
this moment, the whole life of God, with its victory
pain and death.

Let no one draw a wrong conclusion: suffering fo
sake is no privilege; what is privilege—one of the tende
things of God—is suffering for Christ's sake.

Nor is suffering to be courted. It is enough that when
it be conquered; and this not merely by resignation
utilization. When an Indian Brahmin, having turned
but having retained nevertheless a feeling of superio
certain people, was in a crowded bus when it overtu
suddenly discovered that his life was bound up with the
others. His comfortable smugness having been reduced
sense, he was ready to be brotherly toward any man. I
remarked with a smile, "It took a wreck to remake me."
difference between *submitting* to suffering as an in
nuisance and *using* suffering as a permitted beneficence!

'Thus,' says Paul the affectionate to his fellow Christia
will join with me in a constancy of spirit, a firmness o
that will not flee in the face of persecution nor flinch
fellowship of pain. We are together in this, "engaged
same conflict."'

The apostle will write on. His letter is far from fi
Eagerly we shall follow him.

But he has written enough to give us a look inside his
What a heart! What dimensions! What devotion! Ne
think, were the colossal and the compassionate, the titani
the tender, brought together more creatively or fruitfully
here!

III

THE ALERT MAN

III

THE ALERT MAN

THE familiar saying that "An ounce of prevention is worth a pound of cure" may be applied appositely to the letter St. Paul addresses to his friends in Philippi. Herein lies his alertness.

If we may judge from the epistle itself, there was in the collective life of this congregation only one flaw: a threat of division. In the concluding chapter two women will come in for particular mention, and the apostle will urge that the friction between them be brought swiftly to an end. Meanwhile, in ways less personal, he will tell them of the danger in which they stand.

Too extreme, it seems to me, is Professor E. F. Scott's judgment that this church "was broken into cliques, and was vexed with petty questions of precedence."[1] More temperate, and therefore (in this case) more accurate, is Bishop Moule's observation that "their almost only visible defect or danger" was a "tendency to separate somewhat into sections or cliques."[2] Even Professor Scott acknowledges that throughout the epistle Paul "never employs the language of rebuke, as he freely does in other epistles."

So this alert shepherd, seeing the sly approach of the wolf, would make his flock aware of their danger. Already, in positive phrasing, he has said to them: "stand firm in one spirit, with one mind striving side by side for the faith of the gospel" (1: 27). Now he will press this point by letting them know how strongly he feels about it and how confident he is that, given the right use of the resources that are theirs in Christ, they can ward off every threat of friction and division.

[1]Cf. *The Interpreter's Bible,* Vol. XI, Introduction to Philipplans. Nashville: Abingdon, p. 11.

[2]H. C. G. Moule, *Philippian Studies.* London: Hodder & Stoughton, p.15.

I

THE VALUE OF UNITY

"So if there is any encouragement in Christ, any incentive of love, any participation in the Spirit, any affection and sympathy, complete my joy by being of the same mind, having the same love; being in full accord and of one mind" (2: 1, 2).

1. Nothing else than harmony will *confirm Christ's purpose* for them. They must not permit themselves to think that the unity of love cannot be realized or maintained in their midst. Why? Because the strongest reasons may be put forward and the most adequate means may be drawn upon for the attainment of this very end.

Look at them! They are four in number. The apostle marshals them with swift and passionate cogency. He may introduce them by using the word "if," but this is not to suggest the slightest doubt in his mind. It is the rhetorical "if," a device for stressing the utter importance of the matters he is urging.

"Any encouragement in Christ." Is there? Of course. Moffatt's translation is "stimulus." There is the stimulus of His *practice:* He rebuked the trivial bigotry of His disciples who wanted no one casting out devils outside of *their* group, saying to them, "He that is not against us is on our part" (Mark 9: 40).

There is the stimulus of His *prayer*: "Holy Father, keep through thine own name those whom thou hast given me, that they may be one, as we are" (John 17: 11).

There is the stimulus of His *passion*: it was in the presence of Gentiles—those Greeks who came up to the feast at Jerusalem—that He said, "And I, if I be lifted up from the earth, will draw all men unto me" (John 12: 32). And if this does not mean "all men" without *exception* (since some resist the drawing), it does emphatically mean "all men" without *distinction.*

Consider this scene. The year is 1921. The sanctuary is that of Calvary Baptist Church in Washington, D.C. It is Sunday morning. The right hand of fellowship is being given to a class of new members who are uniting with the church. In this class stands Charles Evans Hughes, newly appointed Secretary of State, who is transferring his membership from New York. Beside him stands his little mother. Beside him also stands a Chinese. Said Dr. Abernathy, the pastor, as he glowingly surveyed the group and shrewdly read the minds of his people: "At the foot of the

Cross the ground is *level*!" It is. And *there* is the potent stimulus of Christ toward the unity of His Church.

"*Any incentive of love.*" Is there? Of course. All of the tender persuasiveness of love (for increase of which the apostle was praying in chapter 1) moves in the direction of concord rather than discord. It is perilously easy to waste words when we Christians begin talking about loving each other. Everybody is for it in the abstract. How many of us are for it in the concrete? Forgive the punning, but it's the concrete that is *hard*: the actual person who is so awkward and difficult, the real situation in which the exhibition of love is so taxing.

If we can squeeze sentimentalism out of this, it will be no small gain. Christian love is not the equivalent of *congeniality*. The Christian loves many people whom he doesn't *like*. Carrol Simcox has quarried a sentence from St. Catherine of Siena that is excellently to the point: "The reason why God's servants love creatures so much is that they see how much Christ loves them, and it is one of the properties of love to love what is loved by the person we love."[1] Perhaps you don't see anything lovable in that uncouth, garrulous member of the church who has just been appointed to serve on the same committee with you, but Christ does. Love her for *His* sake and with *His* love.

To be sure, it isn't natural. It is supernatural. That is part of what it means for Him to be living in you by His Holy Spirit.

"*Any participation in the Spirit.*" Is there? Of course. Many have pointed out that the word translated "participation" in the Revised Standard Version, or "fellowship" in the Authorized, may be rendered "partnership." Elder Cumming, however, has worked this out impressively in a chapter he calls "The Communion of the Holy Ghost" in his helpful volume *Through The Eternal Spirit*. In the measure in which we yield ourselves to Him and to the implications of His partnership, we Christians have, through Him, a common *character*, a common *interest*, and a common *work*. The common character is holiness; the common interest is Christ; the common work is labour for the kingdom and glory of God.[2]

The conclusion seems beyond escape: if I am holding attitudes or displaying behaviour that destroys the harmony of the Church, I am despising the partnership of the Holy Ghost.

"*Any affection and sympathy.*" Or "tender mercies and com-

[1]C. Simcox, *They Met at Philippi*. New York: University Press, 1958, p. 67.

[2]J. E. Cumming, *Through The Eternal Spirit*. New Jersey: Revell pp. 185, 186.

passions,"[1] as Professor Erdman translates it. Do these too belong to the purpose of God for those who now are threatened by misunderstandings and tensions? Indubitably they do.

Both toughness and tenderness have a place in our lives. It is getting them mixed up that works mischief. Let him who is tough-minded towards himself and tender-minded towards his fellows be praised. By the grace of God he is enriching the harmony of the congregation. But if the day dawns when he begins being tender with himself and tough on the brethren, look out! He will need not praise but prayer.

Christ and His encouragement, love and its persuasiveness, the Holy Spirit and His partnership with us, compassion and its tenderness—these belong to the purpose of God for us as co-members of His household.

2. But now a further consideration calls us. If nothing less than harmony will confirm the purpose of God, nothing less than harmony will *complete the pleasure of His servant,* the apostle. "Complete my joy!" (v. 2).

How?

Well, if I may adapt the fine phrasing of Dr. Ozora Davis in his handling of these four segments of the first verse, (1) by being of the same mind, (2) by cherishing mutual love, (3) by cultivating harmony of spirit, and (4) by following one master purpose.[2]

Paul had at times to engage in controversy with his own brethren. Yet we can say of him, it seems to me, that he had no fondness for contention. His accent was on unity. When unity was broken, his heart broke with it. When unity was strengthened, his soul sang.

But now we must see that this alert counsellor has no illusions about our demonstrating the value of unity *unless,* far beneath it, is laid a foundation of costly Christian grace.

II

THE VIRTUE OF HUMILITY

"Do nothing from selfishness or conceit, but in humility count others better than yourselves. Let each of you look not only to his own interests, but also the interests of others.

[1] C. Erdman, *An Exposition: The Epistle of Paul To The Philippians.* Philadelphia: Westminster, p. 68.

[2] Cf. O. S. Davis, *Comrades In The Great Cause.* New York: Association Press, p. 37.

Have this mind among yourselves, which you have in Christ Jesus, who, though he was in the form of God, did not count equality with God a thing to be grasped, but emptied himself, taking the form of a servant, being born in the likeness of men. And being found in human form he humbled himself and became obedient unto death, even death on a cross. Therefore God has highly exalted him and bestowed on him the name which is above every name, that at the name of Jesus every knee should bow, in heaven and on earth and under the earth, and every tongue confess that Jesus Christ is Lord, to the glory of God the Father" (2: 3–11).

1. Think first of humility as a *requirement*: "Do nothing from selfishness or conceit, but in humility count others better than yourselves." Sometimes a tale is better than a treatise. There is the story of that day when a friend called on Dr. Alexander Whyte in Edinburgh. This friend had been to hear a lashing sort of evangelist who was conducting a mission in the city. Part of the sermon consisted of strong personal censure directed against certain prominent pastors of the city. "Do you know what he said?" reported Whyte's friend. "He said that Dr. Hood Wilson of the Barclay was not a converted man." Dr. Whyte leaped from his chair, his face suddenly dark with indignation. "The rascal!" he exclaimed, "the rascal! Dr. Wilson not a converted man!" The visitor, amazed to see the man of God so flamingly indignant, went on: "That wasn't all he said, Dr. Whyte. He said that you were not a converted man either!" Whyte's pacing suddenly stopped. The flame in him subsided. Slowly returning to his chair, he put his face in his hands, and remained a long minute in silence. Then, looking up, he said to his visitor, in a voice of impressive pleading: "Leave me, friend; leave me! I must examine my heart."

This "humblemindedness," for which our apostle had to coin a word, is the opposite of self-assertiveness. Being the antithesis of self-mindedness, it becomes "others-minded," able to look not only to its "own interests, but also to the interests of others" (v. 4).

We need not be starry-eyed in our understanding of what is here described as a requisite Christian humility. I do not think Paul is asking for an attitude that habitually disparages one's abilities or decries the status one is given by his fellows. Such a pose indeed is too often a cloak for hiding an actual vanity. The modesty Christ induces, according to Paul, is (1) an honest sense of unworthiness and (2) a conscientious refusal to push oneself ahead of others, especially when, by so doing, strife is generated, factionalism is fostered, and the church is cleft hither and yon by a spirit that cries, "I am of Paul!" . . . "I am of Apollos!"

Somehow we must have an answer to Tersteegen's cry:

"My vile affections crucify,
Nor let one darling lust survive!
In all things nothing may I see,
Nothing desire or seek, but Thee!"

Without this required humility, the modes and forms, the strategies and tactics, of ecumenicity will never succeed.

2. Beyond humility's requirement is humility's *root*: "Have this mind among yourselves, which you have in Christ Jesus" (v. 5). In using the phrase "among yourselves" the Revised Standard Version has scholarly support, but it is far from unanimous. I prefer to go along with Vincent, Lightfoot, and others in clinging to the Authorized Version: "in you."

Perhaps two or three variant translations of this pregnant sentence will be helpful. In Moffatt it reads: "Treat one another with the same spirit that you experience in Christ Jesus."

In Goodspeed: "Have the same attitude that Christ Jesus had."

In Weymouth: "Let the very spirit which was in Christ Jesus be in you also."

However, all of these translations make it clear, as they should, that the word "mind" in the Authorized Version and the Revised Standard Version speaks not of our Lord's *intelligence* but of his *disposition.* "Disposition" is in fact the word that is preferred in *The International Critical Commentary*.

To sum up what the apostle has said so far in this section: the root of unity is humility; the root of humility is the *spirit—the moral temper of "othering" oneself*—found in Jesus Christ and shared by Him with you as you allow Him to possess you.

3. Next comes the *revelation* of this Christ-mindedness: "though he was in the form of God, (he) did not count equality with God a thing to be grasped, but emptied himself, taking the form of a servant, being born in the likeness of men" (vs. 6, 7). Phillips has put us in his debt by a fine rendering: "For He, who had always been God by nature, did not cling to His prerogatives as God's equal."

Here we enter the depths. This passage is oceanic, where the fathoms are countless and the tides are measureless. "In the whole range of Scripture," exclaims F. B. Meyer, "this paragraph stands in almost unapproachable and unexampled majesty."[1] And Dr. W. Hersey Davis has called it "the sublimest passage in Paul about the person of Christ."[2]

Nevertheless, the occasion and the meaning of this eloquent outburst are simple and clear. 'Don't forget,' cries Paul, 'that in all this wide universe and in all the dim reaches of history there has never been such a demonstration of self-effacing humility as when the Son of God in sheer grace descended to this errant planet! Remember that never—never in a million aeons—would He have done it if He were the kind of Deity who looks "only to his own interests" and closes His eyes to the "interests of others!" You must remember, my brethren, that through your union with Him, in living, redemptive experience, this principle and passion by which He was moved must become the principle and passion by which you are moved.'

Think of *the exaltation He enjoyed*: "He was in the form of God" (v. 6). Our English word "form" scarcely captures the richness of the Greek. This is "form" neither in the sense of *material shape* nor *seeming likeness.* The deeper, inner meaning of it is perhaps approached when, for example, we say of a tennis player or a cricketer, "He was in fine *form* today." The subtle thing we really mean to convey is that something belonging to the very essence of this man's game *shone through* in his playing. To Christ, as the second person of the Trinity, belongs the very nature of God.

Belonging also to this exalted state of being was His "equality with God," a phrase which speaks not so much of *nature* as of *relationship.* Such is the Greek construction here that we may take Paul to mean either that this "equality" was His by perfect right and fitness (and not by the slightest presumption) or that it was something on the retention of which He would not insist but would rather forgo in "the interests of others." The second meaning seems to fit best into the total context.

Think, too, of *the reputation Christ renounced*: "but emptied himself" (v. 7). The Revised Standard Version and Moffatt prefer this more literal rendering of the Greek. Weymouth has it, "He

[1] F. B. Meyer, *The Epistle To The Philippians.* London: The Religious Tract Society, p. 81.

[2] Cf. R. A. Herring, *Studies in Philippians.* Nashville: Broadman Press, p. 67.

stripped Himself of His glory." Phillips is similar: He "stripped Himself of all privilege."

How far did this self-renunciation go, this "self-disglorification," to use the extraordinary phrase of P. T. Forsyth?[1]

To His deity? Did he empty Himself of that? No. How *could* He if this indeed is His "nature"?

To His knowledge? Did He empty Himself of omniscience? In the sense of accepting limitations upon it, Yes. For we are told that He "increased in wisdom" (Luke 2: 52) and that He was found saying, "But of that day and that hour knoweth no man, no, not the angels which are in heaven, *neither the Son,* but the Father" (Mark 13: 32). However, the mind of the Church, historically and evangelically, has held that this limitation of knowledge did not imply intellectual incompetence or error.

To His sinlessness? Did He divest Himself of that? Clearly, No. On the other hand, non-temptability? Clearly, the answer is Yes. For He was "in all points tempted like as we are, yet without sin" (Hebrews 4: 15).

Of what then did He empty Himself? The poet's answer is best, since this whole passage is in fact more of an adoring rhapsody than it is a paragraph of systematic theology. Let Milton be our poet:

"That glorious Form, that Light insufferable

. . . . .

He laid aside: and here with us to be,
Forsook the courts of everlasting day,
And chose with us a darksome house of mortal clay."

Think next, Paul bids us, of *the identification Christ accepted:* "taking the form of a servant, being born in the likeness of men" (v. 7). So voluntarily reduced in status is He that the towel takes the place of the sceptre, and He whose right it is to be served by a legion of angels bends low to wash the feet of a dozen men. True, this was "my servant" of Isaiah 52: 13, of whom it was said, He "shall prosper, he shall be exalted and lifted up, and shall be very high." But before that happy end is reached it will be said of Him that "his appearance was so marred, beyond human semblance, and his form beyond that of the sons of men" (52: 14).

[1]P. T. Forsyth, *The Person and Place of Jesus Christ.* New York: Eaton & Mains, p. 300.

We must see something else. Our Lord's identification of Himself with the life and labour of a bondservant rests upon a still deeper identification, which is described in the words "the likeness of men." The word "likeness" does not suggest anything artificial about our Lord's humanity. It does suggest that His humanity gives Him a true community with men but not a complete identity. That is to say, He is *really* human but He is at the same time *more* than human. As Professor Donald Baillie reminds us, *"The Church has never taught that the human element in Jesus, His manhood, is consubstantial or co-eternal with God, but that it is consubstantial with ourselves and belongs to the order of created things."*[1]

Thus, in the paradox of the Incarnation, the *mysterium Christi,* we have the union of the divine and the human, the eternal and the temporal, the sovereign and the servant, the infinite and the finite.

"Come now and view that manger—
The Lord of Glory see,
A houseless, homeless stranger,
In this poor world for thee—
There see the Godhead glory
Shine through that human veil;
And willing, hear the story
Of love that's come to heal."[2]

Or, think of *the humiliation Christ endured*: "he humbled himself, and became obedient unto death" (v. 8). Having already assumed, by accepting the limitations of human birth, the nature and status of a "servant," there is now, in His conscious, developing human mode of life, a voluntary self-abasement.

Look at Him—this amazing Jesus! He is helping Joseph make a yoke in that little carpenter's shop at Nazareth. This is the One who, apart from His self-emptying, could far more easily make a solar system or a galaxy of systems.

Look at Him again! Dressed like a slave, with towel and basin for His menial equipment, He is bathing the feet of some friends of His who, but for their quarrelsomeness, should have been washing *His* feet. Yet apart from His self-emptying and self-abasing, He is no servant, but the Master of an army of servants —angels in white livery who rejoice to fly at His beck and nod.

[1] D. M. Baillie, *God Was In Christ.* New York: Scribner's, p. 150.

[2] J. N. Darby, used by H. C. Hewlett in *The Glories of Our Lord.* Glasgow: Pickering & Inglis, p. 40.

"He humbled himself!" 'Don't forget this,' cries Paul to these dear friends of His at Philippi. 'Don't forget this when the slightest impulse arises to become self-assertive and self-seeking, and so to break the bond of your fellowship with one another!'

Think, finally, of *the crucifixion He endured*: "even death on a cross" (v. 8). When we read that our Lord "became obedient unto death," we see that He stooped to *mortality*; but when we read the phrase "even death on a cross," we see that He stooped to *ignominy*.

We know of course that God cannot die. One writer, grappling with this fact, says that "God become man can die."[1] The sentence is well intended, but it surely is inaccurate. If God in fact *becomes* man, what you have is *man*, a statement that would never have satisfied the apostles or the makers of the Nicene or Athanasian Creed.

What is true is that the God-Man, Jesus Christ, in the perfect union of the divine and the human natures, has a *mode* of existence in which one of the many acts which it is possible for Him to choose is the act of dying. And this He chose! "Therefore doth my Father love me, because I lay down my life, that I might take it again. No man taketh it from me, but I lay it down of myself" (John 10: 17, 18).

But granting this, it yet remains true that He might have died by means less cruel and loathsome than that of crucifixion: by poisoning, for example, by decapitation, or by stoning. Cicero, speaking of punishment by crucifixion, said, "No adequate word can be found to describe so execrable an enormity."[2] Yet it was by this means, according to St. Paul, that "Christ hath redeemed us from the curse of the law, being made a curse for us; for it is written, Cursed is everyone that hangeth on a tree" (Galatians 3: 13).

With this brush-stroke, "even death on a cross," the portrait of our Lord's self-abasement is complete.

"Still, O soul! the sign and wonder
Of all ages see—
Christ, thy God, the King of glory,
On the Cross for thee."

All of this—this entire process of the self-abasing of our Lord—forms what we may call the humility-image. What produced

[1] C. E. Simcox, *They Met At Philippi*. New York: Oxford, p. 73.
[2] *In Verrem*, 5.66.

the image and what perpetually throbs through it is a quality of mind that, incredibly enough, we Christians may have as our Lord lives masteringly in us. This—and nothing less—is the key to Christian unity.

4. What follows is the *reward* of humility: "Therefore God has highly exalted him and bestowed on him the name which is above every name" (v. 9). Was it not our Lord Himself who said, "He that humbleth himself shall be exalted"? (Luke 14: 11). He thus becomes the supreme illustration of this law of God's kingdom.

Is there not a lovely breath of meaning exhaled from the fact that, whereas *He* humbled Himself, it was the *Father* who exalted Him? The resurrection is part of it, of course. The ascension is part of it. The enthronement as the ever-living Mediator is part of it. The ever-widening circle of those who give their faith and fealty to Him is part of it. And immeasurably more that runs beyond our ken and rises above our wit!

The two huge honours that impress St. Paul as he surveys Christ's exalted state are (1) what God does in *bestowing* on Him a name and (2) what men do in *blessing* that name.

It seems a pity that in a passage so lofty in mood and matter there must be any disagreement as to what this "name" is. Lightfoot is confident that it has nothing to do with any particular designation, as "Jesus," or "Lord," or "Jehovah." "Name" here means dignity, fame, and honour. It is *reputation* and not *appellation* that towers in Paul's mind. So some expositors feel.

Maclaren, on the other hand, moves me deeply when he pleads for an interpretation that makes this name none other than "Jesus." My heart speeds up as I hear Maclaren say: "The simple personal name ('Jesus') was given indeed with reference to His work, but had been borne by many a Jewish child before Mary called her child Jesus, and the fact that it is this common name which is exalted above every name, brings out still more strongly the thought already dwelt upon, that what is thus exalted is the manhood of our Lord."[1]

Whichever meaning is preferred, it is safe to assume that Paul is here echoing the twin facts that this whole passage was known to the primitive Church as a hymn of adoration and that the words "Jesus is Lord" constituted the simple, original Christian creed. The precise and ponderous phrases that belong to the great Creeds came later. Valuable as they were, and are, they

[1]A. Maclaren, *Expositions of Holy Scripture*, Vol. 14. Grand Rapids: Eerdmans, p. 262.

are the finely chiselled products of the formal theologian; whereas St. Paul catches up, and rolls along, the magnificent music of the Church's singing heart, the thrilling rhythm of its marching feet.

> *"Lo, in resurrection glory,*
> *Thou art throned in heaven above,*
> *Where Thou dwellest in the fulness*
> *Of the Father's changeless love—*
> *Love bestowed on Thee unmeasured,*
> *Ere the heavens were begun,*
> *Love of God the everlasting,*
> *To His everlasting Son."*[1]

The other honour that rests upon our Lord as the reward of humility is the recognition by others of the name bestowed upon Him by the Father. The name He bestows is the name they bless.

But who are "they"? From the three phrases, "in heaven," "on earth," and "under the earth" (v. 10), some have concluded that Paul refers to angels, men and demons. Perhaps. Again, perhaps not. It is more likely that he has in view the universal acknowledgment, in one form or another, of the sovereign rule of Christ over all creation and the supreme distinction of Christ as the One—the utterly necessary and utterly sufficient One—"whom God hath set forth to be a propitiation" for our sins (Romans 3: 25).

> *"Now to ages of the ages,*
> *Crowned with honour Thou shalt be;*
> *All the heavenly hosts unceasing,*
> *Glory, might, ascribe to Thee.*
> *Fadeless this Thy royal splendour,*
> *Purchased by Thy precious blood;*
> *Thine the praise of every creature,*
> *Holy Son and Christ of God."*[2]

This is the peak of magnificence to which we have ascended!

But let us not forget our starting point. There are those threatening frictions and factions among the Christians at

[1] H. C. Hewlett, *The Glories of Our Lord,* Glasgow: Pickering & Inglis, p. 105.
[2] Ibid., p. 106.

Philippi. The unity of the brotherhood in love stands in peril. The peril would pass, however, if it could be seen that underneath unity is humility—the seeking not only of our "own interests, but also . . . the interests of others."

For us Christians, declares Paul, there is no place where this principle of effacing self in behalf of others appears so impressively as in Christ. He is God giving Himself away, yet remaining God. He is God putting off a sovereign's vesture for a beggar's rags. He is God rising from His bench where He sits as judge and going to the gallows for the criminal. He is God impoverishing Himself, beggaring Himself, exposing Himself to evil's spite and spittle, never sparing Himself until He has made the rude Cross on Jerusalem's hill the sign and the sum of His utter self-giving.

But this is the end of common sense, we say. Of course it is. It is more staggering than that: it is the end of religion. This is salvation. This is the Gospel. This is the new life. This is the new being who lives this life only in the measure in which the humble mind of Christ dwells in him, dominates him, Christianizes him.

Here, then, is the sovereign formula for unity in the congregation, the sovereign answer to every threat of disunity; the virtue of humility, the disposition of self-effacement.

Thus far in the chapter an alert Paul has (1) pressed the value of unity and (2) portrayed the virtue of humility.

What remains?

III

THE VOICE OF RESPONSIBILITY

First, *the voice speaks through Paul:*

"Therefore, my beloved, as you have always obeyed, so now, not only as in my presence but much more in my absence, work out your own salvation with fear and trembling; for God is at work in you, both to will and to work for his good pleasure.

"Do all things without grumbling or questioning, that you may be blameless and innocent, children of God without blemish in the midst of a crooked and perverse generation, among whom you shine as lights in the world, holding fast the word of life, so that in the day of Christ I may be proud that I did not run in vain or labour in vain. Even if I am to be poured as a libation upon the sacrificial offering of your faith,

I am glad and rejoice with you all. Likewise you also should be glad and rejoice with me" (2:12–18).

"Wherefore!" The Christian logic of free grace is always the logic of obedience. From the fact that in His self-humiliation Christ became "obedient unto death" (v. 8) the apostle argues that Christians are bound to accept the responsibility for obedience in carrying out the holy meanings of their salvation.

Says the voice of responsibility: *God's salvation is yours—work it out!* "Your salvation" is the Holy Spirit's phrase. Let us not be afraid of it. It is evangelically correct, we feel, to say that salvation, from start to finish, is *all* of God. This indeed is the way *we* feel. It is the way we should feel. "Not unto us, O Lord, not unto us, but unto thy name give glory" (Psalm 115:1).

But how does *God* feel about it? Does He not know that we cannot be saved without Him? Our answer is Yes. Does He not know also that He will not save us without us? I think our answer again should be Yes. In all the mystery of sovereignty and freedom, election and response, justification and condemnation, approbation and reprobation, let us try always to remember that the God of the Bible is a moral being working with moral creatures in a moral order of realities, in which He never treats a single one of us as a puppet or a mechanism, *always* as a morally responding being of whom He *always* says, "I have set before you life and death... therefore choose life" (Deuteronomy 30:19).

Salvation—our union with Christ in a new life of release from the powers of sin and death—must, as Professor Wuest puts it, be carried out "to its ultimate conclusion."[1] Specifically, in the case of the Philippians, it must be carried out (even though St. Paul is not physically present to watch over them) in an obedience to the "mind of Christ" that will mend their slightly rifted relations and maintain their appropriate unity.

Nor is this a light matter. The carrying out, in every facet and field of life, of the high meanings of our salvation is a responsibility under which we may well tremble. "Work out your own salvation with fear and trembling." "With a nervous and trembling anxiety to do right," is Lightfoot's comment.[2] This, it seems to me, overdoes it. It suggests a posture that is

[1] K. S. Wuest, *Philippians In The Greek New Testament*. Grand Rapids: Eerdmans, p. 73.
[2] Ibid., p. 116.

frightened and fidgety. Phillips, on the other hand, has caught it excellently: "with a proper sense of awe and responsibility."

A surgeon, picking up something I had said in a sermon, remarked to me that, after a quarter of a century of experience in the operating theatre, he still feels the tension of concern and uncertainty every time a new case of surgery confronts him. This fear, reaching its peak while he is "scrubbing up" and being gowned, subsides into calmness as he takes his instrument in hand. This is wholesome. This is becoming. This is the antidote to professional vanity and to a dangerous complacency.

Here, it seems to me, is our clue to the frame of humble fear in which we set about as Christians to interpret our salvation in a hundred daily tasks, through a hundred daily tests.

But now, if constructive fear keeps us from perilous self-confidence in the working out of our salvation, a confident faith keeps us from paralysing self-despair. "For," says the apostle, "God is at work in you, both to will and to work for his good pleasure" (v. 13). Your out-working is matched by His in-working.

Your out-working, while it is yours as to responsibility, is not yours as to resources: it is His. Wuest translates it, "For God is the One who is constantly putting forth His power in you."[1] This power, moreover, works at such a deep level and to such far perimeters of your life that it accounts both for *prompting* and *performing*. What an utterly sufficient God He is: He gives the *desire* to please and the *dynamic* by which the desire is realized!

Was it not Augustine who cried, "Lord, give what Thou askest and then ask what Thou wilt"? Does our faith grasp this? Do we believe—and do we act on the belief—that the gracious God who lays responsibility *on* us works *in* us by His Spirit to enable us to discharge our responsibility? The desiring and the doing, the willing and the working—these are of Him. But they are of Him *for us*.

Two men were talking about their "partying" the night before. One said, "You know what funny things will happen when you get five or six cocktails in you." The narration that followed was stupid and sordid. God be thanked, the Christian can say, "You know what *fine* things happen to you when you get the Holy Spirit in you!" It is then, and only then, that the Christian may, as St. Paul puts it elsewhere, "please him who hath chosen him" (2 Timothy 2: 4).

Thus we have listened to one accent of the voice of responsibility: God's salvation is yours—work it out.

[1]K. S. Wuest, *Philippians In The Greek New Testament*. Grand Rapids: Eerdmans, p. 75.

But there is something further.

Says the voice of responsibility: *God's splendour is yours—let it shine.* A clause in verse 15 provides us with our key: "you shine as lights in the world." "You shine like stars in a dark world," is Moffatt's rendering.

Luminous lives! This is what Christians are to give to the world. It is part of their responsibility.

Consider the *significance* of the Christian's shining, or, collectively, the shining of the Church, amid society's darkness. Jesus said to His disciples, "Ye are the light of the world" (Matthew 5: 14). St. Paul echoes this teaching: "you shine as lights in the world." Both statements, however, are meaningless except as we remember that Jesus said of Himself, "I am the light of the world" (John 8: 12).

In our solar system luminaries are of two orders: the order of the sun and the order of the moon. The sun is a source of light. The moon is not. The light of the moon, as every schoolboy knows, is the borrowed and reflected light of the sun. The moon by itself is a dead, lustreless planet. Only when its face is so related to the sun that it catches the sun's light to the full does it light up with that rounded beauty which makes poets reach for their pens and lovers for the hands of their loved.

This, I suggest, puts us on the right track for understanding Paul's figure. Christ is Light, original, essential, central, eternal; Christians are light, derived, relative, conditional. Our shining is never our own. It is His shining—in us and through us.

This significance grasped, we must see that Paul's heaviest concern here is with the *sphere* of the Christian's shining. It is twofold.

First, there is *the inner sphere of our relationships with other Christians.* Mark the admonition of verse 14: "Do all things without grumbling or questioning." "Questioning," which is the choice of the Revised Standard Version, seems a shade too weak. Vincent observes that usually Paul uses the Greek word here in the sense of "disputatious reasoning."[1]

In some of the churches under Paul's oversight the dissension and strife were intolerable; in the Philippian Church they were merely incipient. There he speaks for the purpose of correction; here he speaks for the purpose of prevention. In the whole of this tender epistle, as we have previously observed, there is no word of open rebuke or castigation.

[1] M. R. Vincent, *Philippians and Philemon,* in International Critical Commentary. New York: Scribner's, p. 67.

It is obviously Paul's purpose to say here: 'Brothers and sisters, "be ever on your guard" (so Weymouth) against grumblings and controversies, for when these profitless activities engage you, whatever else you are doing, you are *not* shining!'

Murmuring! Grumbling! Either one of these is what we call an onomatopoetic word—one in which the sound suggests the meaning. Interestingly, it is the same sort of word in the Greek—*gangusmon.* It is a tell-tale, tonal word. It describes the low mutter of discontent, the mood and the moan of fault-finding.

You remember that murmuring was a sin to which Israel was particularly addicted when they were in the wilderness. They were out of Egypt but not in Canaan. They murmured at the slightest provocation—about their leadership, about their diet, about their wretched circumstances. Ah, these "low grumblings of a man who is swayed by impatient thoughts and hard feelings" have a sad way of taking the shine out of our discipleship.

And there is the "disputing." Let no time be lost in saying that what Paul means by disputing is something much more serious than disagreement. Had he said, "Do all things without disagreeing," it would have been a counsel to which he himself did not live up. He once disagreed with Barnabas. He once disagreed with Peter. He disagreed with the Jerusalem brethren who were of the "circumcision party."

Paul's ban is not on disagreement; it is on ugliness and bitterness of spirit in connection with any disagreements that may arise. The apostle's sombre word to the Corinthians is very much to the point: "For you are still unspiritual; all the time that there is jealousy and squabbling among you you show that you are—you are living just like men of the world" (1 Corinthians 3: 3, Phillips). They were growling when they should have been glowing.

Somewhere I have read that when the Protestant Episcopal Church—our American counterpart of the Church of England—first entered Korea for missionary work, no little difficulty was encountered in finding a suitable and accurate translation into the Korean language of the church's name. At one point in the discussion a translation was proposed which seemed on first examination to be acceptable. Then a doubt arose as one scholar asked the others if they realized what result they would get if they took the suggested words and translated them literally back into English. "Protestant Episcopal Church" would become "Society of Disputing Overseers!"

Well, in my travels I have met some disputatious and domineering souls that would eminently qualify for membership in such a society. May their tribe die out! There's much of defiance about them but little radiance.

Turn now to a second sphere in which Christians are to live luminously. It is the *realm of our relationships with others who are out of the Church and out of Christ.* The phrase that describes this is an arresting one: "in the midst of a crooked and perverse generation." "A warped and diseased world," is the way one version has it. Another reads: "a crooked and perverted age."

The radical evil in man's nature twists the mind as surely as it taints the soul. A moral warp clings, leech-like, to the finest mentality. What is needed is witnesses who are so aglow with Christ's love and truth that the world's crookedness will be shown up for the false and menacing thing that it is. Christian statesmen who are points of light in the political darkness, Christian business men who are torch-bearers in the economic night of greed and exploitation, Christian labour leaders who bring some high candle-power into the murk that often envelopes the "union" movement, Christian educators who will function as floodlights in our cultural twilight, Christian ministers who are not so much intoxicated with theological lore as they are irradiated by Christ's interior and controlling presence—this is what the Church of our Lord should be furnishing to the weary, cynical, bitter world around us.

Once more the voice of responsibility speaks: *God's servant is yours—give him pleasure.*

'Why do I want you to be faithful custodians and communicators of the Gospel, "the word of life"? Because if you fail, you will take from me my *rejoicing* (so the Authorized Version), my *reason to boast* of you (so Goodspeed) when Christ's coming great day shall dawn.' Such is Paul's strong feeling, as expressed in verses 16, 17, and 18.

In the Day of Reckoning if these Philippian converts are standing with him, it will be the thrilling proof that all of his costly ministries and eager exertions in their behalf were not wasted.

For a moment the dear old warrior thinks of the death that may descend on him soon, and he turns that possible event into a splendid and moving metaphor. "Even if I am to be poured as a libation upon the sacrificial offering of your faith," he cries, "I am glad and rejoice with you all" (v. 17). Whether it be the pouring out of wine, or water, or honey, a libation is that which *crowns* the sacrifice.

Paul thinks of the faith and the faithfulness of these converts as an offering made to God. He then thinks of his possible death as a kind of libation in blood that he will willingly pour over their sacrifice, completing and crowning it.

Is not this always, in some measure, the soul-winner's costly hope and gladness? Is not this but another way of saying that the sower in tears looks longingly forward to the day when he will be the reaper in joy?

Rutherford must have felt so when he wrote:

> *"If one soul from Anwoth*
> *Meet me at God's right hand,*
> *My heaven will be two heavens*
> *In Immanuel's land."*

But this puts responsibility on those who have been led into the Way of Life through the witness of God's servants. "You also should be glad and rejoice with me" (v. 18). 'So conduct yourselves, my brethren, that if you hear of my departure, you will have the satisfaction of knowing that I died carrying you in my heart, with your faithfulness to Christ and to me making music in my spirit.'

These, then, are the special accents with which the voice of responsibility speaks through St. Paul. God's salvation is yours: work it out on every broad field, in every nook and corner, of your total experience. God's splendour is yours: let it shine wherever you are. God's servants are yours: give them the pleasure of knowing that their labour of love for you is never a wasted, futile thing.

But *the voice of responsibility speaks again, this time through Timothy:*

> *"I hope in the Lord Jesus to send Timothy to you soon, so that I may be cheered by news of you. I have no one like him, who will be genuinely anxious for your welfare. They all look after their own interests, not those of Jesus Christ. But Timothy's worth you know, how as a son with a father he has served with me in the gospel. I hope therefore to send him just as soon as I see how it will go with me; and I trust in the Lord that shortly I myself shall come also"* (2: 19–24).

We are now at the heart of things—and a very *human* heart it is—in this beautiful letter. Reconstruct the scene. The apostle, soldier-guarded, chain-bound, has two companions: Epaphroditus, who last summer brought a gift and greeting from the Christian assembly in Philippi, and Timothy, who in Paul's eyes is the dearest of friends and the finest of pastors.

The first of these excellent men is about to set out through the rigours of the on-coming winter and the hazards of the perilous journey, bearing this epistle of love to his own fellow-Christians whom he represents. 'Later,' says Paul, 'I shall be sending Timothy, if, as I hope, it is possible to spare him. In the case of each man I am asking you to regard him as having a commission from me. Each will have an important message for you. Each will be deserving of the attentive reception I trust you to give him.'

In this mood the apostle has chiefly three things to say about Timothy, of which they in fact already have some knowledge from his previous labours among them:

1. Timothy is a *sympathetic* man: he will be "genuinely anxious for your welfare" (v. 20). Literally, the vivid and unique word here is "like-souled." It speaks of Timothy's fine capacity to put himself in the place of another. Too often we think of sympathy as something maudlin—a piece of tear-shedding. With or without tears, authentic sympathy means understanding, insight, and with it love's concern to be helpful.

Many a modern ecclesiastic would have sent a subordinate to Philippi to "take a census," or to "do a survey," or to "set up a programme." This man Paul, knowing full well how cold and shallow that procedure can be, wants rather to send a man who knows psychiatry without even knowing that he knows it, who knows the "psychological approach" without ever having to put that bit of trite jargon on display. Timothy knows the difference between *spirit* and *statistics*. "Love," as William Clow once wrote, "is that insight and sympathy that craves to bless and delights to commune." Timothy had it.

"Claim jealous part
In all thy brother's woes,
And wash thy heart
In every tear that flows.
Only by sympathy the spirit knows
Deep things,
And grows
Strong, celestial wings.

The crowned with thorns! God
Make thee one of those;
There are no other kings."[1]

2. Timothy is a *selfless* man: "I have no one like him . . . They all look after their own interests, not those of Jesus Christ" (vs. 20, 21). So sweeping and severe is this sentence that some have accused Paul of a momentary despondency and of that gloomy exaggeration that so commonly accompanies it. This view of the matter I take leave to doubt.

Numerous are the suggestions as to what these strong words really mean. I shall not detail them. Of those who would be possible candidates for such an assignment as this, Paul can think of no one other than Timothy who, immediately present in Rome, would undertake it. If that is startling and disappointing to us (as it must have been to Paul), then let us remember how few there are in *our* churches who carry their dedication right through to the Cross of Christ, where self-interest dies, and the selflessness of total commitment rises white and eager. Where is the Henry Martyn spirit which, waving a gallant goodbye to ease, announces unwhimperingly, "I go to burn out for God?"

This you will find in Timothy. You will *not* find it in the general run of Christians. When you do, you will want to sing a doxology.

3. Timothy, moreover, is a *seasoned* man: "Timothy's worth you know, how as a son with a father he has served with me in the gospel" (v. 22).

There is of course a seasoning that comes with the passing of time and the accumulating of experiences. Yet this may be, even for Christian workers, a highly *individualistic* sort of maturing. One thinks of the notoriously conceited bishop who one night strode across the stage of the auditorium where he was to preach, sat down ostentatiously, and folded his arms with vast aplomb. No novice was he. This was "old stuff" to him. That he was a seasoned "trooper" on the Lord's preaching circuit there could be no doubt. But what a ridiculous individualist he was may be judged by the remark (perhaps unsanctified!) of one observer to another: "Look at him! Did you ever see his like? He can even strut sitting down!"

To grasp the fine sort of seasoning through which Timothy had passed, you have only to seize the little preposition in this 22nd verse: "as a son *with* a father he has served with me."

[1] Frederick Langbridge, source unknown.

Paul might have said, "he has served me." His own modesty and affection ruled that out, fact though it was. "He has served *with* me." He has learned to work in double harness. He knows the meaning of "we." He is no *prima donna*; he is a *partner*.

Have you undergone this kind of seasoning? Some callow pilots do nothing but "solo" flights. It is one stage of the process of becoming a trained flyer. But that captain with whom I rode the other day on an air-liner worth two million dollars and capable of carrying sixty passengers, was no "soloist." He was a "crew" man, working *with* his co-pilot and navigator, and they *with* him.

It is in team-work such as this that all the Pauls and all the Timothys of our Lord's wide and wonderful Church make their finest contribution.

Concludingly, *the voice of responsibility speaks through Epaphroditus*:

> *"I have thought it necessary to send to you Epaphroditus my brother and fellow worker and fellow soldier, and your messenger and minister to my need, for he has been longing for you all, and has been distressed because you heard that he was ill. Indeed he was ill, near to death. But God had mercy on him, and not only on him but on me also, lest I should have sorrow upon sorrow. I am the more eager to send him, therefore, that you may rejoice at seeing him again, and that I may be less anxious. So receive him in the Lord with all joy; and honour such men, for he nearly died for the work of Christ, risking his life to complete your service to me"* (2: 25–30).

In these simple sentences the human qualities of this epistle are again most touchingly evident. Paul moves from the celestial to the terrestrial with a naturalness that we have come to expect in his correspondence, but which appears at its attractive best in Philippians. A moment ago he was writing about such sublimities as the pre-existence and the incarnation of the Son of God and the "madness and elevation of the Cross." Now he writes of the critical illness of a friend and of the concern that this illness would occasion in the hearts of other friends. The sick friend, in turn, has been "distressed" because he has been the cause of anxiety among his comrades in Christ "back home."

The message of *responsible* Christian living in this paragraph is like a stream with two opposing currents: one current flows from the church at Philippi to Paul, the other flows from Paul to the church. Both flow *through* Epaphroditus.

1. *From the church to Paul:* "Epaphroditus my brother and fellow worker and fellow soldier, and your messenger and minister to my need" (v. 25).

"My brother!" My "fellow worker!" My "fellow soldier!" The affectionate eulogy of a noble leader to a noble benefactor!

Many weeks ago he had brought the gift of money which they had collected and placed in his hands for transmission to their beleaguered leader. They made him their "messenger," literally, their "apostle," a word which Bishop Moule says was from the first enriched by the Church with overtones of "sacredness" and "authority."[1]

They made him, moreover, their "minister," literally, their "service-rendering one." Again the overtones are resonant with suggestions of a *sacred* and *public* service. *He* represented *them* in a service of love that lifted Paul's burden by meeting his need.

Thus the current of responsible helpfulness flows from the church to its leader.

2. *From St. Paul to the church:* "I have thought it necessary to send to you Epaphroditus . . . I am the more eager to send him . . . So receive him in the Lord with all joy" (vs. 25, 28, 29).

'As you invested him with authority to minister to me in temporal things, so I am giving him authority to minister to you in spiritual things.'

The strong thrust with which this section of the letter closes should not be missed. If any special reason were needed to induce the Philippians to take Epaphroditus to their hearts when he arrives, that reason may be found in the fact that it nearly cost him his life to carry out the assignment they gave him. The circumstances are not given. What is reported, nevertheless, is that "he nearly died for the work of Christ, risking his life to complete your service to me" (v. 30).

"Not regarding his life" is the rather flat, colourless rendering of the Authorized Version. "Risking his life," is better. In the Greek it is a sixteen-letter word that occurs nowhere else in the New Testament. It is the term for gambling. Here is God's gambler, who many a time had watched the soldiers or the sailors throw their dice and make fools of one another, casting down his life in a magnificent recklessness of love. All for you! All for me!

Above all, for Christ!

[1] Cf., *Philippians* in "Cambridge Bible for Schools and Colleges." Cambridge: University Press, p. 80.

IV
THE ASPIRING MAN

IV

THE ASPIRING MAN

PROFESSOR JAMES STALKER, in his *Life of St. Paul,* reminds us that what we know of the apostle comes to us from two sources: the picture of him given by Luke in the Acts and the portrait of him that forms in our minds as we read his letters. Of the two it is the letters that give us the most vivid unveiling of Paul himself. Says Stalker: "In no other literary form could we, to the same extent, in the writings have got the man."[1] If Paul had massed the truth God revealed to him in one impressive treatise on theology, we should then have seen the truth-loving *mind* of a remarkable thinker. As it is, what we see in his letters is the Christ-possessed *manhood* of a remarkable leader.

Again and again we have been reminded of our thesis in this series of studies. It is that nowhere in his writings does this human quality in Paul have such free and fascinating play as in the epistle to the Philippians. Let me here remind you of another, and closely related, thing: if we have observed Paul the *man* breaking through in the foregoing sections of this letter, we must prepare ourselves for a far more detailed self-portrait in the chapter now before us. Chapter 3 is mainly a piece of autobiography.

The Pauline heart into which we are now permitted to gaze is an astonishing combination of rest and restlessness, of serenity and striving, of deliverance and discontent, and—if you will pardon the awkwardness—of perfectedness and perfectionlessness. But more of this as the chapter unfolds!

I

THE APPROACH THAT IS MADE

"Finally, my brethren, rejoice in the Lord. To write the same things to you is not irksome to me, and is safe for you.

[1]J. Stalker, *Life of St. Paul.* New York: Revell, p. 95.

"Look out for the dogs, look out for the evil-workers, look out for those who mutilate the flesh. For we are the true circumcision, who worship God in spirit, and glory in Christ Jesus, and put no confidence in the flesh. Though I myself have reason for confidence in the flesh also. If any other man thinks he has reason for confidence in the flesh, I have more: circumcised on the eighth day, of the people of Israel, of the tribe of Benjamin, a Hebrew born of Hebrews; as to the law a Pharisee, as to zeal a persecutor of the church, as to righteousness under the law blameless. But whatever gain I had, I counted as loss for the sake of Christ" (3: 1–7).

We have, to start with, a word of *apology*: "rejoice in the Lord. To write the same things to you is not irksome to me, but is safe for you" (v. 1).

What is meant by "the same things"? Some say that it refers to the apostle's repeated emphasis on Christian *unity.* Others regard it as an allusion to the heavy stress on the theme of *joy.* Both of these interpretations have advocates who hold that Paul had written previously to this church, sounding this note of unity or of joy.

Not to be ruled out is the view of some that this opening apology refers not to what has been said but to what is now going to be said. Thus Vincent paraphrases: "I am not backward about writing to you concerning a matter of which I have spoken in former letters, but I am moved by my anxiety for your safety to refer to it again."[1]

However we construe these opening words, it is pastoral concern that breathes through them. Responsibility justifies repetition.

Next comes a word of *admonition*: "Look out for the dogs, look out for the evil-workers, look out for those who mutilate the flesh" (v. 2). Paul is neither angry nor bitter, but he is both bold and blunt. The man who, earlier in his letter, displayed a broad tolerance toward those who preached Christ from partisan and insincere motives now roundly denounces those "Judaizing Christians" who insist that everyone must first become a Jew before he can become a Christian. Paul was unyielding at this point. To say, for example, that a man must be circumcised in order to be a Christian is to pervert the Gospel and poison the minds of those who hear it.

Those who encourage this false teaching are likened to the

[1]Those wishing to pursue this further may consult Bishop Lightfoot's *Epistle To The Philippians*, pp. 138 ff. Grand Rapids: Zondervan.

pariah dogs of the East which, half-wild, are scavengers They call themselves Christians but they are, alas, still feeding cn "the garbage of carnal ordinances," to use Bishop Lightfoot's vivid metaphor.

Furthermore, they are "evil-workers." Their operations and their influence have the evil effect of distorting and debasing the Christian Gospel.

This warning with a triple sting in it concludes by branding these false teachers as "self-mutilators," which is the term Weymouth employs to reproduce, rather literally, the word that is translated "concision" in the Authorized Version. According to Paul's Gospel, a sinner's acceptance with God rests solely on his faith in the crucified and risen Christ. When, therefore, he depends on physical circumcision to give him "privileged status with God," he is so far mistaken that the "cutting" should be in fact regarded as nothing but the mutilation of the body.

Does Paul's admonition have relevance today? Does it hit home to any of us?

Sadly enough, Yes! For "works-righteousness," in some form or another, is a human conceit that is terribly hard to kill. Reasons for this—man's pride being what it is—are not far to seek.

Religiously, man wants to feel *safe* and he wants to feel *superior*.

Take the craving for safety. If salvation can be laid out for us in a pattern of "do's" and "don'ts," if religion is something that can be managed, something manipulable, then by following the prescribed course—by doing this and refraining from doing that—I can earn from God and His ecclesiastical representatives what I want. It makes things tidy and snug.

Henry Drummond told of the professor from abroad who one day said to him: "I used to be concerned about religion, but religion is a great subject, and I was busy, and there was little time to settle it for myself: so I became a Catholic, and instead of dabbling any longer in religion myself, just left it to the Church to do everything for me. Once a year I go to Mass."[1]

Or, to move closer to ourselves in Protestant circles, there were the relatives of the young woman who married outside of her strictly *immersionist* denomination. The pastor who told me of the case said that a very dim view was taken of the spiritual

[1] Quoted by J. S. Stewart in *The Gates of New Life*. New York: Scribners, p. 55.

future of this girl who had dared to cross into another denominational fold. However, a note of cheer entered the conversation when someone gave out with the bright and reassuring exclamation: "Well, at least we can be thankful that she has been *properly* baptized!" Other hazards galore might beset and befall, but in this at least she was safe: she had been baptized by the right *mode*.

Closely related to safety, through the exact application of religion's externalism, is the superiority that one readily comes to feel. If you have done it, or it has been done for you, you have a privileged status. This is eminently desirable. This is ego-soothing. This is flattering.

There is a story—apocryphal, I dare say, and strictly modern—about a hard-working monk of the Carthusian order, who was explaining to a stranger the differences between the several orders of monks. "In learning," said he, "we are not in a class with the Jesuits. The Franciscans excel us in good works. The Dominicans are much better preachers than we are. But when it comes to humility, we're tops!"

Here is peril that surrounds us all. If we deny it, we but heighten the charge that we *are* imperilled. We want to glory in something other than Jesus Christ our Lord: in a denomination that makes us proud; in a ritual whose nice execution makes us feel, "See, how faithfully I do it!"; in our scholarly minister, who as one parishioner put it, "never makes me feel uneasy"; in our mode of dress; yes, even in our precise doctrinal correctness.

And all the while the judging Word of God keeps saying, "He that glorieth, let him glory in the Lord" (1 Corinthians 1: 31). Let him know that saving goodness is always the gift of God and never the achievement—even the *religious* achievement—of His creatures.

We pass next to the word of *affirmation*: "For we are the true circumcision, who worship God in spirit, and glory in Christ Jesus, and put no confidence in the flesh" (v. 3).

As physical circumcision was an authentic mark of the men of Israel, so circumcision of the heart—God's gift of grace, in response to faith, by which we are placed in the "new covenant"—is the distinctive characteristic of the Christian.

This Christian person, or, thinking corporately, this Christian church, has three distinctive characteristics:

1. There is a distinctive *ritual*: "we worship God by the Spirit" (Phillips). I follow those translators who see here a reference to

the Holy Spirit. Christian worship does not despise forms, and cannot indeed dispense with them, but it never relies on them. Its reliance is upon the vitality and potency of the Spirit of the living God. He takes the forms and *informs* them—pours into them the strength of living conviction and the warmth of genuine emotion.

2. There is, besides, a distinctive *rejoicing*: we "glory ('rejoice,' it may be rendered) in Christ Jesus." Whereas some may boast of their legal and external rites, their ceremonies and their ordinances, our boast is in the One on whom the eyes of Isaac Watts were focused when he wrote:

"Not all the blood of beasts,
On Jewish altars slain,
Could give the guilty conscience peace,
Or wash away our stain.

But Christ, the heavenly Lamb,
Takes all our sins away;
A Sacrifice of nobler name,
And richer blood than they."

3. And, to complete Paul's triad of signs, there is a distinctive *renunciation*: "and put no confidence in the flesh." Here, as nearly always in the Pauline writings, "flesh" is used not of the body but of the principle of the self-life. To refine the matter, we should say that here, as in many instances, the *result* is named for the *cause* of the result. If the self-principle has not been crucified in us, we shall fall into the snare of glorying in it by glorying in that to which it clings, which in this case is the rite of circumcision as insisted upon by these "Judaizing Christians." Hence Weymouth translates this final phrase of verse 3: "and have no confidence in outward ceremonies," since these are powerless to secure our salvation.

We are marking, let us remember, the steps that the apostle takes in his approach to the main movement of his thought in this chapter. Thus we come, finally, to the word of *acknowledgment*: "Though I myself have reason for confidence in the flesh also." What follows is Paul's way of saying that if anyone could lay claim to religious privileges and performances, on the basis of which God's acceptance and favour might be gained, he was that one.

By doing a bit of condensing and summing up, we are entitled to say that four species of pride stand out in this man's list of the "credits" that were his in his pre-Christian days:

There is pride of *ancestry*: "circumcised on the eighth day" (no "Johnny-Come-Lately" to the fold of Israel, but a member of the covenant-community from birth), "of the people of Israel" (belonging to the progeny of a prince), "of the tribe of Benjamin" (the sturdy little tribe whence came Israel's first king), "a Hebrew born of Hebrews" (no mixed blood, since both parents were Hebrews).

Do you ask for high religious and racial breeding, for that something that is often called "background"? Paul had acres of it! And the day was when he was fiercely proud of it.

Secondly, there is pride of *orthodoxy*: "as to the law a Pharisee." Pharisees were not all like those pious rogues whom Jesus so drastically denounces in the 23rd chapter of St. Matthew's Gospel. They were the custodians of true and undiluted teachings of Moses and stood, therefore, in opposition to the Sadducees, who, with a lot of scepticism in their system, denied such doctrines as that of angels and the resurrection. "Contending earnestly for the faith" was what the Pharisees made their responsibility, "the faith" being understood, of course, in its Old Testament sense.

A prideful orthodoxy, whether of the Old Testament or of the New, is never in itself a base on which to stand for acceptance before a holy God. When orthodoxy is lifeless, it is arid; when it is loveless, it is putrid.

Third, there is pride of *activity*: "as to zeal a persecutor of the church." "Works-righteousness" can be both blind and brutal; and even when it isn't brutal, it is still blind. For after all it is *our own* way of earning the fare to heaven. In such a system the more zealous we are the more likely we are to hide from ourselves the vanity that poisons our every movement.

Professor Doremus Hayes, in his vivid and illuminating study of the 13th chapter of 1 Corinthians, reminds us that Phillip II of Spain was indubitably a man who thought he was "doing God's service in persecuting the Protestant Church." He was proud of it, so proud indeed that when he learned of the Massacre of St. Bartholomew's Day in France, he "seemed more delighted than with all the good fortune or happy incidents which had before occurred to him."[1] What a travesty—this

[1] D. A. Hayes, *The Heights of Christian Love.* Nashville: Abingdon, pp. 35, 36.

religious egotism that thrills evilly as it races about in the ferocity of its misdirected activity!

And fourthly, there is pride of *morality*: "as to righteousness under the law blameless." Maclaren is probably right when he remarks that in this clause Paul is "evidently speaking of outward actions and of blamelessness in the judgment of men."[1] The man they once called Saul had kept the Pharasaic rules so well that the most searching inquisitor could not have found fault.

Now, of course, the sulphuric acid that, from the Christian point of view, spoils all is just this: the decency achieved, the conformity to code that is accomplished, is *our own doing.* The fact that it leaves out great patches of wrong within us, which can never be got at by any sort of external conformity, is beside the point for the moment. This is *my* doing and I have myself to thank for it. So, with God sidelined, I am that worst of all lost souls: the soul that is lost without knowing that it is lost.

'All of this multiform pride was once mine,' says Paul. 'I was in a position where I could urge it as the ground and right on which I stood for justification before God.'

So ends the introduction to this chapter: an approach that has ranged from stern warning against those who have misplaced confidence in the externals of religion to a frank look at the assets in which the apostle himself might have rested self-confidently.

We pass on now to the main business of the chapter.

II

THE ASPIRATION REVEALED

"Indeed I count everything as loss because of the surpassing worth of knowing Christ Jesus my Lord. For his sake I have suffered the loss of all things, and count them as refuse, in order that I may gain Christ and be found in him, not having a righteousness of my own, based on law, but that which is through faith in Christ, the righteousness from God that depends on faith; that I may know him and the power of his resurrection, and may share his sufferings, becoming like him in his death, that if possible I may attain the resurrection from the dead.

[1] A. Maclaren, *Expositions of Holy Scripture,* Vol. XIV. Grand Rapids: Eerdmans, p. 324.

"Not that I have already obtained this or am already perfect; but I press on to make it my own, because Christ Jesus has made me his own. Brethren, I do not consider that I have made it my own; but one thing I do, forgetting what lies behind and straining forward to what lies ahead, I press on toward the goal for the prize of the upward call of God in Christ Jesus. Let those of us who are mature be thus minded; and if in anything you are otherwise minded, God will reveal that also to you. Only let us hold true to what we have attained.

"Brethren, join in imitating me, and mark those who so live as you have an example in us" (3: 8–17).

Let me first single out the three pivot-points in this passage where the apostle's ardent aspiration is, let us say, *announced*:

Verse 8: "that I may gain Christ."

Verse 10: "that I may know him."

Verse 11: "that . . . I may attain the resurrection from the dead."

When each of these is examined in its immediate context, it will be seen that its leading idea is lit up by a metaphor, either employed or implied. In the first one we shall find the metaphor of the *market-place,* in the second the metaphor of *friendship,* and in the third the metaphor of a *race.*

Consider the first. The words "that I may gain Christ" do not mean 'that I may acquire Him,' though this of course is implied. They mean, rather, 'that I may discover in Him my true wealth as contrasted with these futile things of which I once made so much.'

Hence we have in Christ the gain of a new *perception.* "But whatever gain I had" (in my noble ancestry, my meticulous orthodoxy, my fiercely zealous activity, my silk-smooth, self-won morality), "I counted as loss for the sake of Christ" (v. 7). Here, you see, is the metaphor of the market: the place of profit and loss.

That day, of Damascus fame, when the living Christ broke through the incredible blindness of Saul of Tarsus' soul, a whole world of changed insights and values came swimming into view. On what is salvation based? For men who are radically self-centred, as men *are* everywhere, it rests not within themselves nor upon their doing. It is based upon God's doing: God's deed of grace in the death and resurrection of Christ, which are seen to be *for* us and, rightly understood, *instead of us.*

To *see* this, to see it so compellingly that the vision is shattering and revolutionary, becomes, if I may without shocking you borrow a phrase from Nietzsche, the "trans-valuation of all ancient values." Nietzsche, to be sure, spoke thus in bitter condemnation of Christianity, insisting that the really manly virtues of *power* and *aggression* and *self-reliance* were cancelled out by the Cross and its message of suffering love, and meekness, and grace.

For a Christian like St. Paul, the scale of values has been so radically altered that the old outlooks are simply non-existent and the old assets lie like a rubbish-heap at one's feet. Listen to a pertinent word from John Ruskin: "I believe that the root of every schism and heresy from which the Christian Church has suffered has been the effort to earn salvation rather than to receive it; and that one reason why preaching is so ineffective is that it calls on men oftener to work for God than to behold God working for them."[1] This root of heresy was forever plucked from St. Paul's soul on that day when, as he puts it in verse 12, "Christ Jesus . . . made me his own."

It may be objected by someone that Paul is here witnessing to the new perception of values that suddenly came to him at his conversion. Is he not, therefore, interpreting a past experience rather than testifying to a continuing desire?

The answer seems clear: he is doing both. The repeated use of the word "counted" is instructive, for in the first instance (v. 7) it is past tense and in the second instance (v. 8) it is present: "whatever gain I had, I *counted* as loss for the sake of Christ. Indeed I *count* everything as loss because of the surpassing worth of knowing Christ Jesus my Lord."

"I counted" describes the attitude he took at conversion: no confidence in the flesh; all confidence in Christ.

"I count" describes the attitude he maintains from day to day: no confidence in the flesh; all confidence in Christ.

Advancing now to verse 9, we discover that, beyond the gain of a new perception, there is for Paul the gain of a new *position*: "and be found in him, not having a righteousness of my own, based on law, but that which is through faith in Christ."

"In him!" Those who have made a special study of St. Paul's teaching on the union of the believer with Christ (Professor James Stewart, for example) tell us that this phrase—"in Christ," "in the Lord," "in him"—is used by the apostle not less than 164

[1]Quoted by W. M. Clow, *The Cross in Christian Experience.* New York: Doran, p. 114.

times. "Paul declares his conviction," says Stewart, "that in Christianity the final stress must ever fall on one thing, and on one thing only, union with Christ, life in fellowship with Christ."[1]

Now when our apostle describes his passionate longing to be "found in him," let us not imagine that he is thinking of some far-away event, such as the Day of Judgment. He aspires to be "found in him," as Bishop Moule expresses and interprets it, "at any moment of scrutiny or test; alike in life, in death, and before the judgment-seat."[2]

When I use the phrase "a new position," as suggestive of what Paul means by being "in Christ," let me make it clear that I regard with some alarm the facile way in which modern evangelicals make a kind of fetish out of what we might call "positionalism." The bland and breezy way in which we manage to sort out what is "positional" from what is "experiential," what is to be set down as "union" and what is to be reckoned as "communion," would probably make St. Paul groan if he were to enter some of our evangelical gatherings today.

I should not like to be misunderstood. That these much-used terms have in them a measure of truth I do not doubt. It is my fear, nevertheless, that we have made clichés out of them. It is my further fear that in the case of those terms which are held to describe the believer's objective position, as distinguished from his subjective experience, we often run dangerously close to settling for a theological fiction in place of robust New Testament reality.

What most strikes me in the Pauline treatment of these matters is the bringing together of these two elements of the redeemed life so that what we have in fact is a living blend of both. And all of it—"in Christ!"

What proves *chronically* that a man is out of communion with His Lord proves *convincingly* that he is also out of union. What it says as to whether he was ever in union or not will vary with our doctrinal premises. Into this I need not enter. My concern here is not to inflame controversy. It is to protest complacency. It is to caution against substituting verbiage for vitality. "Not having my own righteousness" are not words to be so construed that I think of Christ, by means of *His* righteousness, merely cloaking the reek of my own character. Maclaren rightly says,

[1] J. S. Stewart, *A Man In Christ*. London: Hodder & Stoughton, p. 153.

[2] H. C. C. Moule, *Philippians*, in "Cambridge Bible Series." Cambridge: University Press, p. 91.

by way of comment on "the righteousness from God that depends on faith": "It is not only 'imputed,' as our fathers delighted to say, it is 'imparted.'"

To be "found in him," means, if we may continue with Maclaren, that this "transforming Presence laid up in 'the hidden man of the heart,' will be like some pungent scent in a wardrobe which keeps away moths, and gives out a fragrance that perfumes all that hangs near it."[1] Blessed position, this! And the soul of this apostle aspires to the moment-by-moment maintenance of it.

Let me sum up what has been said about the first thrust of St. Paul's aspiration: "that I may gain Christ." The figure of speech, we have noted, is that of the market-place. When Paul was captured by Christ, there took place what Jowett calls a "revising of the balance-sheet" as regards profits and losses.

As Jowett splendidly puts it, Paul is "abundantly willing to lose the thin and fading robe of reputation if only he can gain the splendid and incorruptible garment of a sanctified character. And that splendid garment is not the product of works, the fashion of human hands; it is the workmanship of God, the finished creation of His abounding grace."[2]

Come now to the second metaphor under which Paul puts forward the intense and incessant longing of his soul. The figure is that of *friendship*: "that I may know him and the power of his resurrection, and may share his sufferings, becoming like him in his death" (v. 10).

It is clear, for one thing, that in this aspiration there is a craving to know the *person* of Christ. "That I may know *him*!" To *know* a person is much more than to *know about* him. Precisely this distinction, simple as it is, needs to be kept in mind where Jesus Christ is concerned. Just as we truly know music by hearing it and know the light of day by seeing it, so we genuinely know Jesus Christ by responding to His claims and offers and thus allowing Him to reveal Himself to us as tender forgiver and faithful friend.

Recently I was struck by the testimony of a young British doctor. In college he was a famous "rugger," or football player, as we say in the United States. He was also an amateur boxer. He says: "Christ had been nothing to me but a name, when it was put to me that I needed forgiveness, power, and union with God for life to be truly adjusted." After receiving Christ as his

[1] A. Maclaren, *Expositions of Holy Scripture*, Vol. XIV. Grand Rapids: Eerdmans, p. 333.

[2] J. H. Jowett, *The High Calling*. New York: Revell, p. 131.

Saviour and finding that his life was suddenly inundated by a flood of new desires, new motives, new attitudes, new assurances, he made this statement: "A doctor, I feel, needs to be more than an assistant of nature in the healing of body and mind; he needs to be personally acquainted with the One who heals body, mind, and spirit. Not just a medical man and a psychologist, but a disciple as well!"

Certainly! For, while *knowing about* has value, *knowing* has vitality.

But we must now move to a deeper level. We descend to it when we recognize that our personal introduction to Christ is followed normally by a craving for personal fellowship with Him that expands and deepens through all the years. At this point I should like to have you associate with the phrase, "that I may know him," a clause that occurs in verse 12 which, incidentally, receives a dim and ambiguous translation in the Authorized Version. "That I may apprehend," says the Authorized, "that for which also I am apprehended of Christ Jesus." The Revised Standard Version, in my judgment, does scant justice to the vividness of the Greek. Phillips is better: "grasping ever more firmly that purpose for which Christ grasped me." Weymouth is very direct and lucid: "striving to lay hold of that for which I was also laid hold of by Christ Jesus."

Now let us try to reconstruct the "scene," if I may so express it, in Paul's mind at the moment that he wrote these words to the Philippians. It is as though he were saying: 'A long time ago, my brethren, I was placed under arrest! The Lord of Glory, in the mighty person of His Holy Spirit, came down and seized me. He put His hand on my shoulder that day, outside the Damascus walls, and He said, "Saul of Tarsus, you are under arrest! You are My man!"'

Then Paul seems to add, 'During all these years I have been living to carry out the purpose for which Christ laid hold of me. I now reveal to you, my Philippian friends, what that purpose was and is.'

Here let us pause. If you are a Christian today, do you know why Christ seized you in His love and saved you by His grace? Are you quite sure? If you are like many Christians, you will say, when asked this question, "Why, of course I know! He has claimed me for His own in order that He might save me from the doom of hell!" Or, as others would put it, "He has claimed me for Himself in order that He might rid me of my guilt!" Or, as still others would put it, "He has claimed me for Himself in order that He might break the grip of the past and make me a new kind of person!"

Let us suppose that St. Paul were present, listening to all of this. I am afraid he would shake his head in disappointment. He would say to us, 'All these are indeed desirable things. All these, indeed, Christ does for us. Yet all these fall far short of the real end for which He has redeemed us. That end is simply and sublimely this: that we may "know him!"'

The depth and reach of this little phrase are staggering. To know His *gifts* is good, but this is more. To know His *creatures* is good, but this is more. To know His *blessings* is good, but this is more. To know His *comforts* is good, but this is more.

In one of Archbishop Fenelon's letters, compiled under the title of *Christian Perfection,* that saintly soul exclaims:

> "But who does know Thee, O my God? He who wishes to know only Thee, who wishes no longer to know himself, and to whom all that is not Thee will be as though it did not exist. The world would be surprised to hear these words, because the world is full of itself, full of vanity, of deceit, and empty of God. But I hope that there will always be souls who will hunger for God, and who will relish the truths which I am going to say . . .
>
> "Why didst Thou create all these things? They were all made for man, and man was made for Thee. That was the order which Thou didst establish. Woe to the soul who reverses it, who wishes all for himself, and who shuts himself up in himself! This violates the fundamental law of creation. No, my God, Thou canst not cede Thine essential rights as Creator. That would be to degrade Thyself. Thou canst pardon the guilty soul who has outraged Thee, because Thou canst fill it with Thy pure love. But Thou canst not stop being opposed to the soul which takes Thy gifts to itself, and which refuses to relate itself by a sincere and disinterested love to its Creator. Only to fear Thee is not to relate ourselves to Thee. On the contrary, it is only to think of Thee for our own sakes. To love Thee simply to enjoy the advantage to be found in Thee, this is to relate Thee to self, instead of relating self to Thee. What must we do then to relate ourselves entirely to the Creator? We must renounce ourselves, forget ourselves, lose ourselves, enter into Thy interests, O my God, against our own."

It is this insatiable God-hunger that is forever revelling in Jesus Christ. Here is the questing Christian soul caught in the delectable paradox of satisfaction and searching—forever satisfied with Christ and yet forever searching for more of Him!

"There are heights of sweet communion
That are all awaiting me;
There are ocean-depths of mercy
That are flowing full and free;
There are precious pearls of promise
That can ne'er be priced in gold;
There's a fullness in my Saviour
That has never yet been told."[1]

Move now to the next clause in verse 12. Expanding the metaphor of friendship, Paul tells us that his longing to know the person of Christ includes also an ardent desire to know the *power* of Christ: "and the power of his resurrection."

Neither the historic fact of Christ's resurrection nor the prophetic fact of the Christian's resurrection is in Paul's mind here. What is in view is the dynamic fact of the believer's spiritual oneness with the risen Christ, with all that this implies of exhaustless energy that may be tapped for the carrying out of God's purposes both by the individual Christian and by the Church as a whole.

If we get a grip on this thrilling truth, it will change our vocabulary. The trite and trashy things that some Christians say will be heard no more from their lips. If, for example, it is suggested that a Christian ought to be forgiving toward one who has terribly and unjustly wronged him, there are church members galore who are ready to say that such a noble course is just more than can be expected of human nature. The absurd thing about such a statement is its blindness. The whole Christian life is more than can be expected of human nature. The Gospel is revealed in Jesus Christ to persuade wretched human nature to sign its own bankruptcy papers and to let the super-natural power of God take over the receivership, and make something successful out of it.

The trouble with our age is that it is fascinated by just two kinds of power, while it overlooks a third kind, which is far and away the most important of all. Broadly speaking, our age is

[1] Quoted by J. S. Holden in *The Gospel of the Second Chance.* New York: Association Press, p. 109.

enamoured of *mechanical* power and *man* power. The mechanical power is what we see in contrivances that range all the way from the electric toaster on your breakfast table up the scale, through dynamos and Diesels and jet turbines, to atomic bombs. The man power is what may be seen in the human genius that operates, say, a giant corporation, or a political machine, or a totalitarian state.

While these forms of power are roaring or strutting, as the case may be, we are largely neglecting a still higher energy. Man and his machines will eventually destroy his civilization. It is *God-power* that we so mightily need—the sort of healing, redemptive, kindling energy that flows from the heart of the risen Christ through the hearts of His surrendered disciples. In the letter that he wrote to the Ephesians, Paul speaks of it as God's "mighty power, which he wrought in Christ when he raised him from the dead," and he assures the Ephesian church that it is "to usward who believe" that the "exceeding greatness" of this power comes (Ephesians 1: 18–20).

I heard Starr Daily speak some time ago. He makes no claim to being a theologian, and some of us might pick flaws in the way he says things. At the same time one is bound to see in him a miracle of the grace of God. Here is a man who years ago was filled with hate. Bitterness corroded his soul as he languished in prison. Body and mind, he belonged to the Devil, to the underworld of evil. But into that cell seeped the love of God in Jesus Christ. It softened him, broke him, won him, transformed him. The Christ of resurrection, whom Paul once called "the power of God," drained out the acids of hate and revenge and funnelled in the nectars of kindness and forgiveness. Thanks to the "power of his resurrection," Starr Daily went out from prison to broadcast the witness of Christian release and to spread spiritual radiance around the world.

It was this potency of Jesus Christ that Paul had experienced in his own life. It was this that he had seen at work in the lives of others. It was this, moreover, that he longed to have flowing through him continuously giving him just such confidence as later would be expressed in one of our gallant hymns:

"Let troubles rise, and terrors frown,
And days of darkness fall;
Through Him all dangers we'll defy,
And more than conquer all."

Consider, finally, how Paul's aspiration, under the metaphor of friendship, included the longing to know the *passion* of Christ: "and the fellowship of his sufferings, being made conformable unto his death."

Mr. Robert Laidlaw, of New Zealand, whose tract entitled *The Reason Why* has been circulated around the world, remarks that in his travels he has been in homes where a motto was displayed, bearing the words "Saved to serve." He adds, however, that nowhere has he ever found, in home or shop or church, a motto which reads, "Saved to suffer." Yet St. Paul had such a motto—at least on the wall of his mind. In chapter 1 of this letter we have heard him say to the Philippians, "unto you it is given in the behalf of Christ, not only to believe on him, but also to suffer for his sake."

"I long to share His sufferings," is the way Phillips renders it. This aspiration, one fears, exists feebly, if it exists at all, among most Christians of the Western world.

If we were to engage in an honest spiritual check-up, there are some questions, I suggest, that we should not leave out, though the temptation to do so would be strong.

Try this one yourself: Am I discontented over the sheer ease in which my life is lived, with so little of pain in it—so appallingly little that even hints of the cost of my identification with the suffering One who hung there?

Or this: Am I disturbed over the lip-service that I pay to democracy and to Christian principles in government, while in all honesty I have to say that I do nothing that is costly to smite this evil of racial intolerance and injustice?

Or this: Am I agitated and challenged by the opportunities I miss to suffer in prayer, at least a little, with the thousands of Christians who are being imprisoned, bullied, flogged, brainwashed, and either killed or injured for life somewhere or another behind the Iron and the Bamboo Curtains?

The third metaphor under which this man's aspiration declares itself must now have our attention. The market-place recedes. The friendship figure passes to the rear. What moves into the focus of our vision is a race-course. What suddenly proves best suited to the apostle's purpose is the language of a hard-breathing runner: "I press on . . . forgetting what lies behind and straining forward to what lies ahead, I press on toward the goal" (vs. 12, 13, 14).

It is important that we see this in its context. In concluding what he had to say under the figure of friendship Paul let it be known that he had his eye on a day of consummation which shone before him with alluring glory: "that if possible I may attain the resurrection from the dead" (v. 11). The "if" was not inserted, we may be sure, because Paul was worried with doubts. At the same time it was not his way to speak presumptuously. *Contingency* and *certainty* are curiously tied together in the Christian's hope. No doctrine of security remains *fully* in touch with the New Testament revelation if it empties of meaning the solemn word: "if we deny him, he also will deny us" (2 Timothy 2: 12). The faithfulness in which *He* persists, even if *we* prove faithless, is faithfulness to Himself, whom He cannot deny.

In any case, this allusion to the far goal of the "resurrection unto life" (John 5: 29), as distinguished from the "resurrection of damnation," sets Paul's mind going under a new metaphor. He sees himself in the role of a runner. There is a race. There is a goal. There is a prize. Slack souls are ill-fitted for this race. It is a summons to the ardent.

But see now what this modest, honest man does. Having alluded to the perfect blessedness ahead of him at the resurrection, and with full knowledge of the thirty years during which he has been "on the stretch" toward this gleaming goal, he says, "Not that I have already obtained this" (the completeness of the resurrection-state and that higher communion with Christ which it will make possible) "or am already perfect" (with a "perfectedness" which has passed beyond an *approximation* to a *realization* in the day when "this corruptible puts on incorruption"[1] and we no longer "see in a mirror dimly" but "face to face"[2]).

Let us say that in these words of verse 12 we have *a disclaimer that rules perfection out.* But observe *what* perfection this is which must always be disavowed as pertaining to the present life. It is the completeness associated with a finished life and character. More, it is an *order* of perfection in which glorification has crowned sanctification—a body beyond death's reach, a mind with powers immeasurably heightened, the soul's discipline ended, and the luxury of being non-temptable ravishly begun.

'Let none of you think,' says the apostle, 'that I fancy myself *now* to be a possessor of these qualities of perfection. As *prospects,* they claim me; as *possessions,* it would be fantastic for me to claim them.'

In the next breath, however, a towering testimony is raised, the significance of which has not always received the attention it deserves: "but one thing I do . . . I press on toward the goal" (vs. 13, 14).

[1] 1 Corinthians 15: 54. [2] 1 Corinthians 13: 12.

"One thing I do!" Ponder it well. If in the preceding statement there is a disclaimer that rules perfection out, here, I suggest, is *a declaration that brings perfection in.* That is to say, perfection *of a kind*: relative and not absolute, developing and not static, a derivative of divine grace and not in any sense a display of human goodness.

Soren Kierkegaard wrote a remarkable book which bears the title, *Purity of Heart Is To Will One Thing.* You will not necessarily agree with every sentence the intense Dane writes, and you will probably miss, as I do, the figure of Christ clearly drawn (though He is admittedly there in the background), but what you cannot miss is the powerful *motif* of the book, booming in every chapter like the ceaselessly recurrent ocean surf, namely, that the Christian heart is pure only as it has renounced all double-mindedness and has begun to "will one thing": the "Good in truth"—God!

Kierkegaard ends with a prayer:

> *"So may thou give to the intellect, wisdom to comprehend that one thing; to the heart, sincerity to receive this understanding; to the will, purity that wills one thing. In prosperity may thou grant perseverance to will one thing; amid distractions, collectedness to will one thing; in suffering, patience to will one thing."*[1]

Do we not find ourselves reaching back to a prayer in the Psalter that we have read many times? "Teach me thy way, O Lord; I will walk in thy truth: *unite* my heart to fear thy name" (Psalm 86: 11). F. B. Meyer has a chapter on it in the book he calls *The Soul's Pure Intention.* The chapter is entitled "The Undivided Heart." Is it an empty phrase? Or does it enshrine something tremendously real?

One thinks of the testimony of William Hunter, one of the contemporaries of John Wesley, who after several years in the Christian life passed through a spiritual crisis that brought a significant inner unitedness in place of dividedness. Having struggled long, as he put it, with "many things within me which opposed the grace of God," he then testifies:

> *"I found unbelief taken away out of my heart; my soul was filled with such faith as I never felt before; my love to Christ*

[1]S. Kierkegaard, *Purity Of Heart Is To Will One Thing.* New York: Harper & Brothers, p. 205.

was like fire, and I had such views of Him as my life, my portion, my all, as swallowed me up. . . . A change passed upon all the powers of my soul, and I felt a great increase of holy and heavenly tempers."[1]

Someone, I fancy, is certain to say, "But that is a 'Methodist' way of speaking, and the followers of Wesley have always had this dubious streak of 'perfectionism' in their system." Such a stricture is the more understandable if the objector has had the misfortune of association with a person or group whose want of emotional balance has been exceeded only by the lack of practical consistency. Yet the matter cannot be so lightly brushed aside.

Listen to that distinguished minister of the Anglican Church, Prebendary Webb-Peploe, who for many years thrilled with his scholarly expositions of Scripture the thousands who attended the Keswick Convention in England's "Lake District":

"For many years I was a minister and faithful preacher of the doctrine of justification, but I had no joy for every moment, no rest in the midst of trouble, no calm amid the burdens of this life; I was strained and overstrained until I felt that I was breaking down."

Then came new light from God and the response to it in faith. There was the testimony given to him privately by Sir Arthur Blackwood. There was the illuminated text on the wall: "My grace is sufficient for thee." There was the instant, half-irritated reaction of his frustrated soul, "It is *not* sufficient, it is *not* sufficient!" There was the quiet, desperate cry, "Lord, let Thy grace be sufficient!" There was the rebuking Inner Voice that said, "You fool, how dare you ask God to *make* what *is*?" There was the chastened response, "O God, whatever Thou dost say in Thy Word I believe, and, please God, I will step out upon it." There was the further revealing, reassuring word of Galatians 2: 20, "not I, but Christ liveth in me."

And then—the release! The release from a divided mind and a distracted heart! Said Webb-Peploe: "When the truth came —'not I, but Christ liveth in me'—the rest of faith was practically known in my life."

Here, if I mistake not, is simply another man's way of saying

[1] Quoted by W. E. Sangster in *The Path To Perfection.* Nashville: Abingdon, p. 127.

that he had come, in God's mercy, to the same place in Christ in which Paul stood when he declared, "This one thing I do." It is the strong unity of the heart made *whole*—the undivided mind. And it reminds me of a sentence by P. T. Forsyth, in a little volume called *Christian Perfection*: "Our perfection, therefore, is not to be flawless, but to be in tune with our redeemed destiny in Christ."[1]

The disclaimer that rules perfection out and the declaration that, from another standpoint, brings it in are now followed by *a directive that lights perfection up:* "Let those of us who are mature be thus minded" (v. 15). The Revised Standard Version is warranted in using the word "mature," but in doing so it may mislead readers into thinking that "perfect" in verse 12 and "mature" in verse 15 are different terms. They are not. In the Greek they are identical.

Let us proceed with care. There is a maturity that St. Paul disowns: it is ahead; it brings character to ultimate completeness; it is associated with the event and excellence of the resurrection. At the same time—and here is the paradox in this paragraph which so many readers of Paul have found perplexing—there is a maturity that the apostle, so far from disavowing, clearly claims, and claims for others as well. "Let those of us who *are* mature be thus minded."

I want now to offer another quotation from Forsyth's *Christian Perfection*. Remember that this is from a theologian who greatly fears almost every brand of "perfectionism" that has appeared in the history of the Church. Roman Catholic "perfectionism," where so much is made to depend on deeds of merit, is roundly rejected. The "perfectionism" of Protestant pietism is likewise a peril, he feels. It is too subjective, too individualistic, too self-occupied.

On the other hand, Forsyth is aware that you cannot do justice to the "perfectionism" that *is* in the New Testament if you merely say, "All Christians are 'in Christ,' and Christ is perfect; therefore all Christians are perfect in Christ." That solution is too easy. Now ponder this statement:

> *"It is well to get rid of the idea that faith is a matter of spiritual heroism, only for a few select spirits. There are heroes*

[1] P. T. Forsyth, *Christian Perfection*. London: Hodder & Stoughton, p. 111. The whole discussion by the author is stimulating and provocative, with some phrasings and viewpoints from which I would dissent, but with numerous insights that I have found immensely rewarding.

of faith, but faith is not only for heroes. It is a matter of spiritual manhood. It is a matter of maturity."

Pause here. If Forsyth stopped at this point, with no attempt at running the word "maturity" through a defining process that strains the ambiguity out of it, we should be entitled to say, "There, it is all a matter of *time* and *growth* and *seasoning*." How some Christians do love the nimble nebulousness of "growth"! 'Give us time,' they say, 'and our tempers will be sweet, our worldly-mindedness overcome, and our catty tongues tamed.' And by "time," of course, they mean something conveniently "stretchy."

Have such persons ever examined a New Testament passage like Hebrews 5: 12? Phillips renders it: "At a time when you should be teaching others, you need teachers yourselves to repeat to you the ABC of God's revelation to men! For anyone who continues to live on 'milk' is obviously immature—he simply has not grown up."

Time is not a magic sanctifier. Within its context regression takes place, as well as progression. Bearing this in mind, let us continue with Forsyth:

> "Faith is the condition of spiritual maturity in the sense of adultness, of entering on the real heritage of the soul. It is the soul coming to itself, coming of age, feeling its feet, entering on its native powers. Faith is perfection in this sense. It is not ceasing to grow, but *entering on the normal region of growth*."[1]

This comparative perfection, Paul would have it understood, consists (through faith) of a "mind," or, let us say, *mindedness*, in which, "forgetting what lies behind and straining forward to what lies ahead," we "press on toward the goal for the prize of the upward call of God in Christ Jesus" (vs. 13, 14).

Here, then, is the man whose one claim to perfection lies in nothing he has done but in something that has been done for him. Christ has captured him. The "capture" is centrally so complete that it has *got* him—all there is of him. It has pulled his personality together. It has made half-way loyalties absurd. It has turned the divided mind into the single aim. It has made of him a "this-one-thing-I-do" man.

As for everything else, whether in himself or in his surroundings, the mark of imperfection is upon it. Hence the appropriate-

[1] P. T. Forsyth, *Christian Perfection*. London: Hodder & Stoughton, p. 106.

ness of humility. Hence the necessity of constant vigilance. Hence the demand for the never-ending prunings of the disciplined life. Hence the summons to an adventure in perpetual growth.

Those who take Paul's directive seriously, who are "thus minded" in their spiritual adultness, must take account of two things:

1. This "mind" is one of *perceptive forgetfulness*: "forgetting what lies behind" (v. 13). Obviously this does not mean turning the past into a blank. Besides being impossible (for the normal person), this would be imprudent. It would, moreover, be a contradiction of many a Biblical counsel, such as "*Remember* the sabbath day, to keep it holy" (Exodus 20: 8), or "this do ye . . . in *remembrance* of me" (1 Corinthians 11: 25).

No, total forgetfulness cannot be Paul's meaning. It must be that he is referring to a perceptive and selective forgetfulness.

Your *failures,* for example. Let them teach you, but do not let them terrorize you. As opportunities for development, remember them; as occasions for despair, forget them.

Your *successes,* too, need the discriminating handling of a memory that knows how to forget. Remember them insofar as they make you humbly grateful; forget them insofar as they make you conceitedly self-sufficient.

Thus we see the wisdom hidden in the statement that "a good memory possesses not only the power of recall but also the power of forgetting. It must, however, be a power of selective, as contrasted with haphazard, forgetting."[1]

> *"Old Past, let go, and drop i' the sea*
> *Till fathomless waters cover thee!*
> *For I am living, but thou art dead;*
> *Thou drawest back, I strive ahead*
> *The Day to find."*[2]

2. A perceptively forgetful mind must be also a *passionately forward* mind. In one of my dictionaries the Number 5 definition of "forward" is "ready, eager." That is the sense in which it is used here. Like a glove, it fits the "magnificent obsession" that our apostle describes when he says, "straining forward to what lies ahead, I press on toward the goal for the prize of the upward call of God in Christ Jesus" (vs. 13, 14).

[1] L. Dewar and C. E. Hudson, *Psychology For Religious Workers.* New York: Long and Smith, p. 86.

[2] *Poems of Sidney Lanier.* New York: Charles Scribners' Sons, p. 245.

See the racer speeding toward the finish-line, his eager eyes on the goal, his head thrown forward, his every muscle and motion expressive of the exertions being made to win the trophy. The picture of himself that Paul here presents is no less strenuous than this. The message of the picture should not be missed: the restlessness of faith is as real a component of the Christian life as is its rest. The lure of the *unattained* is as authentic an experience of Christ's disciple as is the assurance of the *given.*

The "end" that keeps calling this man is given a double description. It is called the "goal" (or "mark" in the Authorized Version) and the "prize." "I press on toward the goal for the prize!" Expositors are generally agreed that some distinction exists between the two, though some suggest that it should not be pressed unduly. "It is needless," writes Charles Erdman, "to distinguish between what is symbolized by the 'goal' and the 'prize.' Both refer to that exalted destiny to which God has summoned the apostle."[1]

Canon Guy King appears to favour an interpretation of "goal," or "mark," that has been brought forward by a nineteenth-century commentator, who translates Paul's Greek so as to make it read, "I follow in the course *along the mark.*" This alters the meaning substantially, since it transfers the thought from the finish of the race to its progress, and makes Paul say, 'I am pursuing *the marked-out course.*' The thought is valid enough: if we are Christians at all, we are Christians on Christ's terms, not on our own.

The question is whether this thought can be drawn legitimately from Paul's language. It is probably better to think of the "goal" as the winning line or post, and the "prize" as the garland or wreath of victory that the king or some other dignitary would give to the winner.

If this is the symbolism, what is the meaning of it? I suggest that the "goal" is *Christlikeness.* I use the term as representing the full-blown flower of all our possibilities in resembling the flawless spirit and life of our Master. This, and nothing less, is the predestined end of our redemption: to be "conformed to the image of his Son" (Romans 8: 29).

And the "prize"? Let dogmatism hide its face. My suggestion is open to revision, but I share it for whatever it may yield in insight. It seems to me that we are entitled, at this point, to make more of "the resurrection from the dead" than most inter-

[1] C. R. Erdman, *Epistle Of Paul To The Philippians.* Philadelphia: Westminster Press, p. 111.

preters have done. I would link the "prize" on the one hand with this phrase in verse 11 and, on the other, with what is said in verse 21 about our "lowly body" becoming, in the resurrection, like Christ's "glorious body." We shall carry this thought further in a moment.

Meanwhile, Paul must offer a gentle word—perhaps the more shaming for its gentleness—to those who have not made so total a response to this "high calling of God in Christ Jesus" (v. 14): "if in anything you are otherwise minded, God will reveal that also to you" (v. 15).

'If some of you think that this life of perfection-in-process-of-being-perfected is too lofty and demanding, if you cannot say, "This one thing I do," if past experiences that ought to be forgotten still haunt you, with here a festering resentment and there a daunting failure, if in the confusion of your mind or the discouragement of your heart you wonder why the life triumphant is not yours, God will not leave you frustrated and groping.

'Yet He will do just that unless you keep all of the windows of your soul open to His light.'

This appears to be the import of the obscure words in verse 16, which Phillips renders, "It is important that we go forward in the light of such truth as we have ourselves attained to."

"All light," says Sam Shoemaker, "is binding light, if we see it; no one has authority to make us accept light which we do not see, but we may be wilfully refusing to see it, in which case they (the keen Christians with whom we are prepared to associate ourselves in our quest for God's best) may need to go further back and help us with our stubbornness and self-will."[1]

This is a matter so serious that most of us Christians are giving less than half the attention it deserves. We are looking for the guidance of God that directs us, while shunning the guidance of God that convicts us. We dash about, hither and yon, being, you see, among the Lord's shallowly excited "do-gooders," and all the while His Holy Spirit is seeking to quiet us and subdue us and persuade us to listen. It is that listening openness through which He comes—invasively and pervasively. When a business woman became garrulous and truculent with me because God, in her view of things, had been less than kind or fair to her, I said, "Frankly, I don't know all the answers to your questions, but I am convinced that light will come to you if you will really get quiet before God and listen to His Word." "Get quiet!"

[1] S. M. Shoemaker, *The Church Can Save The World.* New York: Harpers, p. 95.

she exclaimed. "Why, that is the one thing I don't dare to do!"

In the quietness the light we do have becomes strangely luminous and, as we respond to it, more light comes. We should not be surprised if the Holy Spirit goes to work on us by pointing out something we already know: a strained relationship in the family that needs to be relaxed through confession and the humbling of oneself, a call of duty that we have long dodged, a wounded pride that we have not allowed to heal, a nasty temper that has more than once reduced the effectiveness of our witness.

Whatever the symptoms of being "otherwise minded," the Spirit of God will make them evident. Then comes the real test: will we let the symptom-producing disease of an uncrucified self receive from Christ the only cure He has for it, which is *death*?

> *"Go then and learn this lesson of the Cross,*
> *And tread the way that saints and prophets trod:*
> *Who, counting life and self and all things loss,*
> *Have found in inward death the life of God."*[1]

III

THE ANATHEMA THAT IS PRONOUNCED

"Brethren, join in imitating me, and mark those who so live as you have an example in us. For many, of whom I have often told you and now tell you even with tears, live as enemies of the cross of Christ. Their end is destruction, their god is the belly, and they glory in their shame, with minds set on earthly things" (3: 17–19).

Earlier in the chapter Paul has made his readers realize how easy it is to misuse the law by making a letter-perfect conformity to it the basis for our acceptance and approval before God. Legalism opposes grace, and must therefore be renounced if grace is to be received.

The apostle now takes up the painful duty of exposing another false view, wherein not the Jewish *law* but Christian *liberty* is being abused and degraded. After pleading with these younger Philippian Christians to follow the example set by himself and his comrades, Paul turns to a withering denunciation of those

[1]Quoted by J. G. Mantle in *The Way Of The Cross*. Brooklyn: Christian Alliance Publishing Co., p. 75.

whose example it would be fatal to follow. Professing grace, they nevertheless pervert it.

The ban Paul places on these counterfeit Christians is the more terrible because it is so tender. The very destruction he foresees and foretells is drenched with his tears.

In pronouncing this anathema on these "enemies" *within* the commonwealth of believers, five things emerge:

1. *The disguise they wear.* This inference is drawn from the fact that they are called "enemies." They *pose* as the Gospel's friends; they *practise* as its foes. New Testament scholars are not greatly at variance in their opinion as to the character of these abusers of Paul's doctrine of grace. It is generally held that they were "Christians" who became infected with either or both of two errors.

The first was the error that the material world, which would include the human body, is essentially evil, a false philosophy that later ballooned into the huge menace of a movement known as "gnosticism." If the body is incurably evil, why bother to subject it to moral disciplines? That was the twisted logic whose foul seepage was to be found in low living.

The other error was that of mishandling what we commonly call the doctrine of "justification by faith." It consists, to quote Bishop Moule, "of pushing the truth of justification into an isolation that perverted it into a deadly error, and teaching that the believer is so accepted in Christ that his personal actions are indifferent in the sight of God."[1]

These are they who would say, 'Let us sin that grace may abound.' This was abhorrent to Paul, as is clear from his letter to the Romans. Yet this perversion of grace rears its head in every age of the Christian Church. A prominent churchman wrote a kind of "Open Letter" to John Fletcher, in which he said:

> "I am therefore persuaded that, as God did not set His love on me at first for anything in me, so that love, which is not at all dependent upon anything in me, can never vary on account of my miscarriages; and for this reason: when I miscarry, suppose by adultery or murder, God ever considers me as one with His own Son, who has fulfilled all righteousness for me. . . . There are no lengths, then, I may not run, nor any depths I may not fall into, without displeasing Him . . . I may murder with him (David), worship Ashtaroth with Solomon, deny

[1] H. C. G. Moule, *Philippians* in the "Cambridge Bible Series." Cambridge: University Press, p. 102.

Christ with Peter, rob with Onesimus, and commit incest with the Corinthian, without forfeiting either the Divine favour or the kingdom of glory."[1]

If legalism dies hard so does libertarianism! Both are obstacles to any sound understanding of the Gospel of God's grace.

2. *The doom they face.* "Their end is destruction" (v. 19), says Paul, with no mincing of words. "These men are heading for utter destruction" is the even stronger translation of Phillips.

This is seen to be inevitable, as the evidence against them piles up.

3. *The deity they serve.* Whatever pious profession of service to God may flow unctuously from their lips, the fact is that "their god is the belly" (v. 19). This phrasing is not for the fastidious. It is the deliberate coarseness of the Holy Ghost. Bishop Moule is surely justified in saying that the reference is to "the sensual appetites generally" and not exclusively to "gluttony in food."

"The fact is," says Dean Robert R. Wicks, "that we have all been swept along blindly in a movement away from God that began some three hundred years ago under the leadership of science. We have transferred our trust to scientific knowledge, which comes through our senses, because from this source we gained the immeasurable benefits, conveniences, and luxuries which are the essence of modern life."[2]

This is the new idolatry: to make the senses and whatever gratifies them our chief delight and our principal reliance. It is an idolatry that invades the ranks of professing Christians, with a mischief that is all the more menacing for being so stealthy.

4. *The disgrace they bear.* Paul's charge is that "they glory in their shame" (v. 19). Professor Erdman's paraphrase is illuminating: "they pride themselves upon those indulgences which are really their disgrace."[3]

5. *The disposition they display.* "With minds set on earthly things," is the final and the summarizing condemnation of these sham believers. They have a mind-set that is orientated earthward, not heavenward. Their lives are horizontal—all soil and no sky. They wear the Christian label but they libel the Christian spirit.

[1] J. Fletcher, *Checks To Antinomianism,* Vol. I. New York: Phillips & Hunt, p. 259.

[2] R. R. Wicks, *The Interpreter's Bible,* Vol. XI. Nashville: Abingdon, pp. 96, 97.

[3] C. R. Erdman, *Epistle of Paul To The Philippians.* Philadelphia: Westminster Press, p. 115.

England's poet-laureate saw the peril of this materialism in a Christian land, and shot a powerful dart into its cold heart when he wrote:

> *"For heathen heart that puts her trust*
> *In reeking tube and iron shard,*
> *All valiant dust that builds on dust,*
> *And guarding, call not Thee to guard,*
> *For frantic boast and foolish word—*
> *Thy mercy on Thy People, Lord!"*[1]

The poet's insight is sound: this thing-mindedness is heathenish, and not less so because it happens to be the obsession of people whose names are on our church rolls.

All this sternness of indictment and prophesied doom came from a heart that was grieved and aching. It was an exposé done by a man whose eyes were red from weeping. Robert Murray McCheyne and a brother-minister were exchanging thoughts on the sermon each had preached on the preceding Sunday. "This was *my* text," said McCheyne, " 'The wicked shall be turned into hell, and all the nations that forget God,' but," he added, his voice choking, "I preached it with a breaking heart." Paul was like that—tender in thought even when he had to be terrible in theme.

IV

THE ANTICIPATION THAT IS PICTURED

"But our commonwealth is in heaven, and from it we await a Saviour, the Lord Jesus Christ, who will change our lowly body to be like his glorious body, by the power which enables him even to subject all things to himself" (3: 20, 21).

From those who "mind earthly things" the apostle turns to the true representatives of Christ who know that, while they have earth as the *locale* of their discipleship, the real source and centre of their life is higher than anything earthly. It is heavenly.

The figure of speech that Paul here employs would be highly effective with these Philippians. Moffatt has perhaps caught it best: "we are a colony of heaven." Philippi was a Roman colony. Its citizens enjoyed the same status as those of Rome. Philippi was a bit of Rome away from Rome.

'We Christians,' says Paul, 'constitute a spiritual colony, or commonwealth, whose King is not Caesar but Jesus Christ,

[1] Kipling's "Recessional", quoted by permission from *The Five Nations*, Methuen (Canada, Macmillan Co).

whose substance is not "meat and drink, but righteousness, and peace, and joy in the Holy Ghost" (Romans 14: 17), and whose regulative principles are not found in edicts by the emperor or laws passed in the Roman Forum but in the living truth and the luminous authority of Christ the Lord.'

In that anonymous piece of Christian writing of the second century known as the *Epistle To Diognetus* there is this sentence: "Christians, as dwellers, are on earth; as citizens, in heaven."[1]

This mode of thinking needs to be renewed and re-emphasized in every generation. It must not be forgotten that even under nominally Christian governments, like those of Britain and the United States, the Christian Church is a community of faith and love whose ultimate loyalty is not to queen or president, to parliament or congress, but to the Lord of Glory. Its members are those who can say with St. Paul: God "hath delivered us from the power of darkness, and hath translated us into the kingdom of his dear Son" (Colossians 1: 13).

I should feel guilty of being both tactless and thankless if I failed to recognize that our governments which are formed within the Christian tradition do in fact acknowledge that their citizens have an ultimate allegiance to God that transcends all lesser loyalties. When the Honourable Charles Evans Hughes was Chief Justice of the Supreme Court of the United States, a decision was handed down in which the following remarkable words occur: "In the forum of conscience, duty to a moral power higher than the State has always been maintained. . . . The essence of religion is belief in a relation to God involving duties superior to those arising from any human relation."

Think, too, how the hymnody of the Church bears witness to this Pauline vision of Heaven as the true "father land," the real "mother country," of the Christian. Wrote James Montgomery:

"Here in the body pent,
Absent from Him I roam,
Yet nightly pitch my moving tent
A day's march nearer home."

Or there is William Hunter's "Going Home," in which the fourth verse runs:

[1]Cf. *Philippians* in "Cambridge Bible Series." Cambridge: University Press, p. 104.

"Let others seek a home below,
Which flames devour, or waves o'erflow,
Be mine the happier lot to own
A heavenly mansion near the throne."

The Christian is not a settler here. He is a pilgrim. A *pilgrim,* let it be quickly added, and not a *tramp*! A tramp is aimless; a pilgrim has a shrine in his heart and a destination in his eye.

Thus, according to Paul, the Christian is the great anticipator. With Browning he can say, "The best is yet to be!"

What are the components of this forward look? Paul has a threefold answer:

1. There is the *sure return*: "we await a Saviour, the Lord Jesus Christ." Ah, the colonists are expecting their absent king to visit them? Some years ago I was motoring with a friend over a long, long road in central India. For miles on end the trees that bordered that road bore a special mark. My friend explained that this was part of the extensive preparation being made for the arrival of the *Maharajah* of that province. A princely visit was soon to take place. This was part of the recognition that would be accorded him.

The verb that is translated "await," or "look" in the Authorized Version, is a strong one. It has clear overtones of *eagerness* and *intensity*. It is not the waiting of idleness or quiescence, but of alertness and yearning. "Even so, come, Lord Jesus!"

2. There is the *splendid redemption*: "who will change our lowly body to be like his glorious body." How great an improvement is this over the phrase, "our vile body," which has stood so long in the King James Version!

On this let us be clear: neither St. Paul nor any other writer in the New Testament ever held the human body in contempt. He never taught that it was sinful, as did some of the heretical groups in early Church history—the Gnostics, for example.

Paul did indeed teach, what all of us must frankly recognize, that the body has upon it the multiple marks of limitation and weakness, and that these are part of the total testimony to man's fallen and sinful estate. The body is fettered by frailties, locked within limitations, pursued by pain, doomed to death. Paul knew this, and knew it well. Before long they would take him out, lay his neck upon a block, and sever head from body—a body in which, for Christ's sake, he had known hunger and heat, privation and pain, sickness and stoning, weakness and weariness.

That body would lie lifeless on the sands of the Ostian way. Would that be the end of it? Never!

Beyond that scene of death there arose in Paul's vision another scene. Christ would one day return. At His coming Paul's deathless spirit would be clothed with a glorified body, fashioned in power and beauty like the resurrection body of his blessed Lord. Then, in that happy day of consummation, will rise the shout: "O death, where is thy sting? O grave, where is thy victory?" (1 Corinthians 15: 55).

Vincent holds that the prevailing Jewish belief contemplated merely "the restoration of the present body," whereas Paul's inspired idea "includes an organic connection with the present body, but not its resuscitation."[1] It will be a transfigured body. The two Greek words that are translated "change" and "like" are of more than passing interest. The word for "change" means, literally, to *re-scheme*, that is, to redesign the *appearance* of the body. Details of that appearance are withheld. How we should like to know! Paul does indeed tell us, in the *locus classicus* on the resurrection, which is the 15th chapter of 1 Corinthians, that it is "sown," or buried, "in decay," but raised "without decay"; "sown in humiliation," but "raised in splendour"; "sown in weakness," but "raised in strength"; "sown a physical body," but "raised a spiritual body." Such is the Williams translation of verses 43 and 44. Beyond this, what with the reticence of the New Testament, we can but fall back on St. John's word, "it doth not yet appear what we shall be" (1 John 3: 2).

The other Greek word that is singularly suggestive is the one translated "like": "like his glorious body." What the word implies, according to Professor Scott, is that our resurrection body in "its outward appearance, will correspond to its inner nature," and that in this correspondence it will be "similar to the body of the exalted Christ."[2] Agreeable to this fine interpretation, Bishop Moule would add the comment that "the coming conformity to our Blessed Lord's body shall be in appearance *because in reality*; not a mere superficial reflection, but a likeness of constitution, of nature."[3]

'Ah, yes,' cries Paul, 'our King-Redeemer is coming again. The night of waiting may be long, but dawn will break at last.

[1]Cf. *Philippians and Philemon* in the "International Critical Commentary." New York: Scribners, p. 120.

[2]E. F. Scott in *The Interpreter's Bible,* Vol. XI. Nashville: Abingdon, p. 103.

[3]H. C. G. Moule, *Philippians* in the "Cambridge Bible Series." Cambridge: University Press, p. 106.

And His coming will mean, among many things, "the redemption of our bodies"' (Romans 8: 23). And this in turn means that Christ will give us bodies that will adequately serve the purposes of our redeemed spirits. The spirit will then have an organ of expression suited to the holiness of its nature and the happiness of its estate. The prayer of Oliver Wendell Holmes will be answered:

> *"O Father! Grant Thy love divine,*
> *To make these mystic temples Thine!*
> *When wasting age and wearying strife*
> *Have sapped the leaning walls of life,*
> *When darkness gathers over all,*
> *And the last tottering pillars fall,*
> *Take the poor dust Thy mercy warms,*
> *And mould it into heavenly forms."*

3. To the sure return and the splendid redemption Paul now adds, as the third component of the Christian's hope, the *sufficient resource*: "by the power which enables him" (Christ) "to subject all things to himself."

Questions? Of course there are questions. How are the dead raised up? With what body do they come? How can the grip of death ever be completely broken in a world where it has for so long stalked so imperiously? How can the rule of evil be finally and forever broken on a planet where it has wrought its havoc so persistently and malevolently? How can it be that One so mild and yielding as to let men spit in His face and spike Him to a tree shall yet be the one King overruling all other kings, the one Name eclipsing all other names, the one Face outshining all other faces, the Glory out-dazzling all other glories?

The answer, cries Paul, is simply this: "He is able!" This rendering of the Authorized Version strikes the trumpet note that is here most appropriate. This divine ability is brought forward by Paul in language that cascades, in words that tumble over each other. "According to the working of his power" is a good translation of the Greek, but it hardly carries the force that Paul obviously intended. For he uses, in jubilant juxtaposition, the two Greek words for power, the one meaning power in general, the other power in *exercise* or *release*.

No one, I believe, has begun to grasp the message of the New Testament unless he sees at least two tremendous things emerging from its pages. The first is that in the death and resurrection of our Lord—and let it not be forgotten that the two events are really one—the Almighty God has revealed Himself and released His power so directly and overwhelmingly as to constitute a new departure in history. This is creation. It is creation by redemption. It is the shattering of the old creation. It is the beating down and the casting out of the powers of darkness. It is the overthrowing of Satan. It is the invasion, here and now, of "the powers of the world to come."

Nothing less than this would satisfy the mind or interpret the message of the early Church, once they caught the titanic meaning of the resurrection.

The other truth—indissolubly linked with this first one—that gleams and glitters on the New Testament page is this: that not only the Church but the whole world of good and evil is moving now toward a purposed consummation under the Lordship of Jesus Christ; yet this climax is not to be thought of as the *winning* of God's victory in the world made by Him and marred by sin, but rather as the *exhibition* of His victory in Christ. The victory has been already won.

The ultimate outcome, therefore, is never in doubt. Sin *will* be uprooted. Suffering *will* be ended. Disease *will* be banished. Rebellion *will* be put down. Death *will* be hurled into the pit. And

"Jesus shall reign where'er the sun
Doth his successive journeys run;
His kingdom spread from shore to shore,
Till moons shall wax and wane no more."

If we persist in saying, "How can these things be?" the answer stands: "He is able!" There comes a time, as Karl Barth somewhere remarks, when we have to "allow God to be God." The God who is God indeed, the "God and Father of our Lord Jesus Christ," will surely, irresistibly, bring it to pass.

Said the cynical Omar Khayyam: "The stars are setting and the caravan starts for the dawn of nothing."

Said the serenely confident St. Paul: "We await a Saviour, the Lord Jesus Christ, who will change our lowly body to be like his glorious body."

Between the bleak cynicism of the one and the brilliant confidence of the other stands that one tremendous thing that became the exuberant message, the confident *kerygma,* of the Christian Church—the resurrection of the Lord Christ!

In these twenty-one verses the wide-ranging mind of our "aspiring man" has covered an astonishing spectrum of truth:

1. Legalism, or "works righteousness," is hopeless as a basis for justification before God. It must therefore be renounced.

2. Justification by faith and a living union with Christ, while distinct, can never be separated: they are one.

3. In the life of union with Christ we face a paradox: a relative perfection is required—and given—which takes dividedness from the centre of the believer's life and puts unitedness in its place, while at the same time a progressive perfection keeps humbling the believer with the realization of the unattained and urging the believer on to the goal of perfected Christlikeness.

4. Longing both for the reaching of the goal and the "prize" that is associated with it, the Christian, even in the midst of those who are counterfeit disciples, waits eagerly for the "crowning day" and the share that he will have in the final victory of the risen and returning Lord.

V

THE ADEQUATE MAN

"THE art of living," says Dr. E. Stanley Jones in the "Introduction" of his book called *Mastery*, "the art of living is the least learned of all arts. Man has learned the art of existing, of getting by somehow with the demands of life, of escaping into half answers; but he knows little about the art of living, about being able to walk up to life, with all its demands, humbly conscious that he has within him a mastery that is able to face this business of living with adequacy."[1]

"To face this business of living with *adequacy*!"

Not, mind you, with tranquillity, or with security, or with prosperity! There is something bigger, more comprehensive than these: adequacy!

It is precisely this Christian ability to cope with life that shines through so splendidly in the concluding section of this letter. Again the *humanness* of the redeemed life comes to the front. Very human situations must be faced as the affectionate, solicitous, and delicately tactful apostle draws his epistle to a close: friction between two women of the congregation, requiring immediate correction lest a major quarrel rend the fellowship; the gift of money the apostle has received, calling for grateful acknowledgment; the courtesy of Christian greetings from the believers at Rome to their comrades in Philippi, asking for conveyance through Epaphroditus.

No profound theology here, no sublime philosophy—just simple, human considerations glorified by the touch of Christ upon them!

What is more, the treatment of these matters is given an intensely human context. It is Paul the *man*—the man "in Christ" to be sure, but the man nevertheless—whom we see impressively as the agent through whom the Holy Spirit is ministering to these Philippian Christians. We see him as the embodiment of that amazing adequacy for life in all of its

[1] E. S. Jones, *Mastery*. Nashville: Abingdon, p. v.

endlessly varied circumstances. Thus we hear him say categorically: "what you have learned and received and heard and seen in me, do" (v. 9).

This is not immodesty on parade. This is Paul's way of sharing a secret. He has found the way of mastery. It works. He has no doubt of it. He therefore wants his friends at Philippi to possess the same secret.

I

THE ADEQUACY EXPRESSED IN PAUL'S TEACHING

"Therefore, my brethren, whom I love and long for, my joy and crown, stand firm thus in the Lord, my beloved.

"I entreat Euodia and I entreat Syntyche to agree in the Lord. And I ask you also, true yokefellow, help these women, for they have laboured side by side with me in the gospel together with Clement and the rest of my fellow workers; whose names are in the book of life.

"Rejoice in the Lord always; again I will say, Rejoice. Let all men know your forbearance. The Lord is at hand. Have no anxiety about anything, but in everything by prayer and supplication with thanksgiving let your requests be made known to God. And the peace of God, which passes all understanding, will keep your hearts and your minds in Christ Jesus.

"Finally, brethren, whatever is true, whatever is honourable, whatever is just, whatever is pure, whatever is lovely, whatever is gracious, if there is any excellence, if there is anything worthy of praise, think about these things. What you have learned and received and heard and seen in me, do; and the God of peace will be with you" (4: 1–9).

1. Paul interprets to the Philippians a *love* that is adequate.

For one thing, it is a *spacious* love. All are included, the quarrelsome Euodia and Syntyche no less than the helpful Clement. "My brethren" is an inclusive phrase, which transcends all differences of sex or situation.

It is, moreover, a *solicitous* love that the apostle displays. True, they are his "joy" and his "crown," since their kindness to him has already brought him cheer and their presence with him in glory will some day be his laurel-wreath of eternal satisfaction.

Nevertheless, he carries a burden of concern for them. "Stand firm!" This is one part of his burden. The "therefore" links their steadfastness in faith and loyalty with the prospect of

Christ's return which he has just brought before them. As citizens of the heavenly commonwealth, they are to be patriots, with never a shadow across their allegiance to the King.

Does Paul mix his figures of speech? In the preceding chapter he said "run." Now he says "stand." There is no contradiction. As to growth and service, the Christian's posture is never that of standing still: here he is runner. As to faith and loyalty, his position is that of standing: here he is immovable.

Paul's solicitude embraces something more than the firmness of loyalty he wants these Philippians to exhibit. It extends to the fellowship of love he longs for them to manifest. At the time of his writing this fellowship is being marred and seriously imperilled by the strife between Euodia and Syntyche. As to who they were, and what it was that occasioned their friction, we are left in the dark. Speculation on both points has been long and sometimes fantastic, one suggestion being that these were not individuals at all but rather names given to groups, "church parties," that threatened the unity of the congregation.[1]

They were in fact prominent ladies of the church who, for some reason, were not living up to their lovely names. "Euodia" may be translated either "Prosperous Journey" or "Sweet Fragrance," while "Syntyche" may be rendered "Fortunate" or "Affable." Since Euodia's conduct was exuding something other than "fragrance" and Syntyche's reaction was something less than "affable," they needed the tactful counsel and help of Paul's unnamed "yokefellow," who is urged not to let the affair deteriorate into a serious breach, but to mend matters while there was time.

It is the mischievous way of minor irritations in church life to grow into major disputes. The tiny squall becomes a thundering storm. The Holy Spirit's way is to check the mischief at the first ominous puff of an ill wind.

Knowing all this so well, Paul's love for these women and the congregation of which they were a part went out to them in solicitous yearning. Nor was it a love that was fickle and forced. It was eager and persistent. It was ample and constant. The mark of adequacy was clearly upon it.

2. See, next, how Paul interprets to his friends a *joy* that is adequate: "Rejoice in the Lord always; again I will say, Rejoice" (v. 4). Low-mooded and peevish, Voltaire once exclaimed that men are "tormented atoms in a bit of mud, devoured by death.

[1] Cf. H. C. G. Moule, Cambridge Bible on Philippians. Cambridge: University Press, p. 109.

a mockery of fate. This world, this theatre of pride and wrong, swarms with sick fools *who talk of happiness*."[1]

Well, with or without the approval of all the Voltaires in the world, St. Paul talked freely and frequently about "happiness," or, more accurately, about that lilt and lift of the soul that rise above happiness into *joy*. To any for whom the difference is merely hair-splitting, I defend joy as a preference because it does not depend on "hap." Men who make their living by compiling our dictionaries say that "hap" is "luck," chance happening. And if you are "hapless," say they, "it means the unlucky thing has happened." Hence your *un*happiness.

Joy! Abundant joy! Whatever it is, Paul made a great deal of it, "sick fool" though he would have been in Voltaire's eyes. Eleven times he says to these Philippians "Rejoice!" Five times he flings out his mirthful monosyllable, "Joy." Three score and ten times this joy-note is struck in the New Testament.

Joy is the courageous cheerfulness of the Christian soul. If there is abandonment to Christ, and not a reluctant giving of ourselves to Him in pinched little fragments, then two things can be said of the gladness that will be ours: (1) it is *incessant in its song* and (2) *independent in its source.*

"Rejoice . . . *always*!" That makes it incessant.

"Rejoice *in the Lord*!" That makes it independent. Circumstances may be bright or black, the stock market may be up or down, health may be good or bad, friends may be many or few. Regardless, you are "in the Lord" who once took the grim shadows of His cross as the grey setting for these glowing words to His disciples: "These things have I spoken unto you, that my joy might be in you, and that your joy might be full" (John 15: 11).

Thus the joy that Paul experienced—and extolled—must be seen as joy *in spite of*! In spite of a *flogging*: it was at Philippi that he and Silas, beaten to within an inch of their lives, "sang praises." In spite of *fetters*: even as he wrote this love-letter he was held by what he calls in Acts 26: 29 "these chains." In spite of *friendlessness*: a little later he will write to Timothy, saying, "At my first defence no one took my part; all deserted me" (2 Timothy 4: 16).

But the Pauline joy is also gladness *because of*! Not because of prosperity, or popularity, or pleasure, but because its deep and dependable spring is "in the Lord," who, both by the example He

[1] Quoted by W. P. King in *The Search For Happiness*. Nashville: Abingdon, p. 9.

set us and by the motives He supplies us, keeps the soul's blitheness from slipping into boredom.

"In the Lord!"

Charles Wesley knew this song:

> *"Thy mighty name salvation is,*
> *And keeps my happy soul above:*
> *Comfort it brings, and power, and peace,*
> *And joy, and everlasting love.*
>
> *Jesus, mine all in all Thou art;*
> *My rest in toil, my ease in pain;*
> *The medicine of my broken heart;*
> *In war my peace, in loss my gain;*
> *My smile beneath the tyrant's frown;*
> *In shame my glory and my crown."*

3. Paul's next instruction is that there is an adequate *gentleness,* without which the Christian will be needlessly rough and those who know him needlessly wounded: "Let all men know your forbearance" (v. 5). "Have a reputation for gentleness," is the paraphrase of the Greek that Phillips gives.

Reading St. Paul one gains the unmistakable impression that here was a balanced soul. He believed in the beauty of each Christian grace, but he believed also in the symmetry with which these graces are to adorn our lives. Who has not seen the Christian who, although a lion in courage, seems never to have blended this vociferous valour with the lamb-like quality of gentleness? The disciple of the Lord is not apt to utter the impudent or the impure word. It is much more likely that he will speak the impetuous and the imperious word, with a hurt in someone's heart as a consequence!

After all,

> *"The bravest are the tenderest,—*
> *The loving are the daring."*[1]

4. Again, the solicitous apostle wants his Philippian friends to know that Christ has for them an adequate *security*: "The Lord is at hand. Have no anxiety about anything" (vs. 5, 6).

Two decisions in construction and interpretation must here be made. The first: Do the words, "The Lord is at hand," express

[1] Quoted by W. D. Cavert in *Remember Now.* Nashville: Abingdon, p. 111.

Paul's belief in the near and speedy return of Christ or are they intended to convey his implicit confidence in the intimacy and adequacy of Christ's living presence by His Holy Spirit? It may strike some as bold to prefer Canon Guy King and Bishop Handly Moule to Lightfoot and Alford. But this I do. Accordingly, I like the vigour and simplicity of the Phillips rendering: "never forget the nearness of your Lord." The Psalmist's colourful word comes readily to mind: "Thou shalt hide them in the secret of thy presence from the pride of man: thou shalt keep them secretly in a pavilion from the strife of tongues" (Psalm 31: 20).

Years ago, under Stalin, a group of thirty Russian peasants were met in secret for worship. Suddenly their worship was halted by the arrival of the dreaded Stalin agents. The leader ordered one of his men to take down the name of every person in the little assembly. When this was done, an old man spoke up: "There is one name you have not got." "I have them all," snapped the officer. "Believe me," said the aged peasant, "there's one name you do not have." A recount was made, after which the officer said roughly, "I told you so—thirty!" The peasant being still insistent, the officer said impatiently, "Who is it, then? Speak out—who is it?" At which the aged man, with a reverence that matched his courage, replied: "The Lord Jesus Christ! He is here!" "Ah," retorted the officer, sneeringly, "that is different!"

It was different indeed—in a way that Stalin's stooge could not possibly understand. The Lord Jesus, in sober fact, *was* there, utterly real to faith's eye, defending them with a kind of weaponry that munitions-makers have never devised.

Thus we have made our decision in interpretation: *for* the view that Paul has principally in mind the presence now of the living, risen Lord, and, rather than saying *against* the view that he had in mind the second coming of the Lord, let us say *in preference to* this view.

The decision on the point of construction remains. Does the sentence, "The Lord is at hand," belong to what the apostle has already said or to what he is about to say? Dean Alford, whose authority bears tremendous weight, asserts that it can be taken either way. I shall cast a ballot in favour of the second construction.

Thus we may think of Paul as saying, 'Brothers, O brothers, if only you will remember the nearness of your Lord, you need have no anxiety. On the contrary, you may—and you should—"in everything by prayer and supplication with thanksgiving let your requests be made known unto God."'

Here are four things that stand related to this whole matter of the Christian's security in a world of peril and panic, a society of agony and anxiety: (1) the provocation (whatever it is that tempts to worry and fretfulness: family troubles, financial reverses, unemployment, ill health, old age, etc.), (2) the prayer ("let your request be made known unto God"), (3) the praise ("with thanksgiving"), (4) the peace ("And the peace of God, which passes all understanding, will keep your hearts and your minds in Christ Jesus.")

And all this is, of course, linked to the Presence: "The Lord is at hand."

Dr. Alexis Carrel, who rode to fame on the tremendous circulation of his book *Man The Unknown,* wrote an article for the *Reader's Digest,* which carried this testimony:

> "As a physician, I have seen men, after all other therapy had failed, lifted out of disease and melancholy by the serene effort of prayer. It is the power in the world that seems to overcome the so-called 'laws of nature'; the occasions on which prayer has dramatically done this have been termed 'miracles.' But a constant, quieter miracle takes place hourly in the hearts of men and women who have discovered that prayer supplies them with a steady flow of sustaining power in their daily lives."[1]

Now, holding that illuminating quotation in mind, listen to a story that was told me by a friend who was a missionary on the ill-fated ship *Zamzam,* sunk by the Germans in the early days of World War II. The ordeal of being torpedoed, forced to leap into the sea, and then being picked up by the crewmen of the armed German freighter, was enough to strain nerves to the breaking point.

The passengers, a considerable number of whom were missionaries, were separated on the basis of "male" and "female," with the ladies spending the first night aboard in a hold at one end of the ship and the men in a hold at the other. Next morning they were permitted to come "top side" and mingle. "Were you nervous?" "Were you cold?" "Were you afraid?" "Could you sleep?" These were the questions that were being asked and answered. Finally a Lutheran missionary, a veteran of several terms on the field, a spare man who was far older than most of his travelling companions, was asked how he managed to get through the night. The substance of his answer was: "I thought

[1] *Reader's Digest,* March 1941, p. 34.

at first that I couldn't possibly sleep. The floor was terribly hard and, as you can see, I don't carry much 'padding' with me. But then I began communing with the Lord. He reminded me of His word in the 121st Psalm: 'My help cometh from the Lord, which made heaven and earth. He will not suffer thy foot to be moved: he that keepeth thee will not slumber. Behold, he that keepeth Israel shall neither slumber nor sleep' (vs. 2–4).

"I was greatly struck with those words, 'he that keepeth Israel shall neither slumber nor sleep.' So I said, 'Lord, there isn't really any use for both of us to stay awake tonight. If You are going to keep watch, I'll thank Thee for some sleep!'"

"And," said he, "I got it!"

The provocation was there: plenty of room for worry! The praise was there: gratitude for rescue from the sea that might have swallowed him. The prayer was there: simple, unforced, child-like. And, as the physical slumber proved, the peace was there: the unpanicked poise that drew, as by a miracle, upon the fathomless serenity in the Saviour's heart.

Am I suggesting that this is the only understanding of security that the Christian can offer to a reeling world—this highly individualistic experience of the presence and garrisoning of God? Not at all. Let statesmen who are also churchmen, and churchmen who are also statesmen, work at all levels to achieve a reasonable measure of protection against the needless social and economic and military threats of our time.

But let it be clear as a freshly washed pane that all the security in the world, contrived by external arrangements, will never make confident, serene, and shock-proof the soul of a man who has no profound inner confidence in God.

Haven't we demonstrated by now that man-made securities are never more than towers made of tissue-paper? Name them: money, fame, friends, atomic bombs, armies, medicines, hospitals. They are all alike—little expediences to postpone the day when the dark blow is struck.

It is when the blow does strike that the Christian man can say: God is my anchor, not in final resort but in first *and* final resort.

The anchor holds!

Peace!

5. Still thinking of the Christian adequacy that St. Paul would teach younger Christians, let us note, finally, that he wants them to be furnished with an adequate *inspiration*: "What you have learned and received and heard and seen in me, do; and the God of peace will be with you" (v. 9).

There is a double incentive here: first, the inspiration of a personalized *pattern* and, second, the inspiration of a peace-giving *presence.*

Think of the first a moment. The Philippians are reminded that when Paul was with them what they *learned, received, heard,* and *saw* was not a set of abstractions, however lofty and lovely, but a burning consciousness of Christ which the apostle not only talked about but embodied. In Greek culture one of the key words was "virtue," or excellence. Now, says Paul, using this particular word for the only time in all his correspondence, you have seen its several facets in the Gospel I brought to you and in the life-in-Christ which I lived before you.

What is this excellence that Greek philosophers have praised and that the Gospel of Christ makes possible? What are its components? The answer is in verse 8.

"Whatever is true." There is an order of truth and reality that is independent of us because it is grounded in God. Our business is not to conduct a Gallup Poll to learn what popular opinion may be or how it may be shifting. Our business is to make a norm, a standard, out of that reality that we see in God as He stands revealed in Jesus Christ. All truth may be a concern to us, but what is to lure us and lift us and command us is the truth that genuinely reflects the nature of God. Jowett's distinction is relevant: "Truth in a police court is correspondence with fact. Truth in the New Testament is correspondence with God."[1]

"Take Thou our minds, dear Lord, we humbly pray;
Give us the mind of Christ each passing day;
Teach us to know the truth that sets us free;
Grant us in all our thoughts to honour Thee."

"Whatever is honourable." This too belongs to Christian excellence. "Honest," which is the familiar word of the Authorized Version, is not to be rejected out of hand, but it is not a "higl fidelity" word: it lacks the overtones of the Greek, which Matthew Arnold once rendered "nobly serious." Always its rich music celebrates *that which commands respect.* Recall that when Tennyson describes the extraordinary courtesy of King Arthur and Sir Launcelot, he makes it clear that their graciousness, far from being a shallow pretence, was rooted in a certain inward magnificence:

[1] J. H. Jowett, *The High Calling.* New York: Revell, p. 202.

"These two
Were the most noble-mannered men of all;
For manners are not idle, but the fruit
Of loyal nature and of noble mind."

Paul's point is that if Christ is given sway over our minds, the things that are unworthy of our reverence will secure no controlling hold upon us.

"Whatever is just." Some translators would have it read "right" or "righteous." It evidently summons us to give righteousness every appropriate expression in our conduct as Christians. This is not easy, even when the *will to justice* is healthily present. Even *good* things, as we have seen earlier, are not necessarily or in every circumstance the *right* things.

I think most of us admire the Quakers for the love of peace they everywhere display. Yet there are times when the attempt to maintain complete consistency in their pacifism leads to a disregard for this distinction between what is good and what is right. Recently they have been urging, through the American Friends Service Committee, that the United States and other nations cancel "nuclear weapon tests," and that if other nations will not do it, the United States cancel such tests anyhow. Disarmament should be begun also, co-operatively by the big powers generally, if possible; unilaterally by the United States, if necessary. Now all of this is urged on the ground that, according to one of their posters, "it is wrong to prepare to kill other men."

Now let us agree at once that it is good to prepare to help men, not kill them. But this hearty concession leaves the question wide open as to whether it is *always* and *under all circumstances* wrong to prepare to kill. Not long ago I was guest in a home close to which the police force of a large city had a "pistol range." There were men out there practising marksmanship. They were preparing to kill. Viewed within a narrow context, at any rate, their work would have to be so described. Of course, viewed within a wider context, it could be described as preparation to protect the lives and property of innocent and defenceless citizens.

It is not possible, frankly, for us as Christians to achieve complete agreement as to what constitutes "justice" or "righteousness" in every concrete situation in this evil and complicated world. It is possible, however, for us to place ourselves under the Christian obligation to provide the maximum both of what is *good* and what is *right.*

"Whatever is pure." Marvin Vincent's comment on the mean-

ing of the Greek word for "pure" is noteworthy: "Not to be limited here to freedom from the sins of the flesh: it covers purity in all departments of the life, motives as well as acts."[1] The temptations that come to "the pure in heart" will never be met victoriously without the discipline of sound thinking. The suggestions and allurements of evil must be met *first* on the battlefield of the mind. They will be vanquished, immediately or gradually, not by a direct assault upon them but, strangely enough, by inviting onto the field a whole flock of thoughts that are positive and pure: thoughts of Christ and the holy blood of sacrifice shed for us, thoughts of others and the battle *they* may be fighting, and therefore thoughts of the praying *we* may do creatively in their behalf. This procedure is helpful, if for no other reason, because it shifts the centre of attention from ourselves to Christ and others.

"Whatever is lovely." The word for "lovely" may be translated "admirable." What is in view is that which is *love-worthy.* In the depths of our souls we know that there are forms of conduct and qualities of character that we can do nothing but despise—cowardice, for example. We know just as well that there are other aspects of behaviour and traits of soul that we can do nothing but admire—courage, for instance. The free rein that we give to our thoughts should be governed accordingly. Such is Paul's argument.

"Whatever is gracious." A literal rendering would be: "whatever is fair-speaking." Dwell on that which strikes the Christian mind as being attractive, "high-toned," winsome. I know a Christian organization whose name, together with the name of one of its leaders, was fraudulently used to cash a cheque—two cheques in fact—at the counter of a large transportation company. When the cheques were not honoured by the bank, the transportation office notified the office of the Christian organization. The leader of the organization informed them that he had never heard of the man who had cashed the cheques and expressed some surprise that no attempt had been made to verify the man's name and claim before giving him the money. Nevertheless, the Christian group sent that corporation $150.00 to cover the loss, which otherwise would have been taken out of the wages of the employee who had, somewhat carelessly, cashed the cheques. Later this employee told the gentleman who had sent the money for reimbursement that this magnanimous act had made a profound impression on the traffic manager of the company. It was

[1] M. R. Vincent, Philippians and Philemon in *The International Critical Commentary*. New York: Scribners, p. 138.

a piece of graciousness, he recognized, that went beyond the call of duty. It was splendidly praiseworthy. It was so high-toned as to surpass justice and express grace.

See now how Paul gathers up the values found in this pattern of Christian excellence and applies them: "if there is any excellence" (as of course there is), "if there is anything worthy of praise" (as there obviously is), "think about these things" (v. 8).

"Think!" With wry humour, someone has said: "Ten per cent of the people think. Twenty per cent think they think. And the rest would rather die than think." Actually, Paul's word is a strong one. It means to think in the sense of *calculate*, as a builder does when he takes careful measurements before attempting to build. And Dean Wicks' suggestion is provocative. He would paraphrase the apostle thus: "Take account of these things with a view to committing yourselves to them." It is not intended that they should merely be praised but that they should be practised. That small boy who is reported to have said, "The Bible begins with Genesis and ends with Revolutions," should be forgiven his inaccuracy because of the truth he unwittingly announced. Exactly this is what takes place when the Bible is taken seriously: there is the kind of "revolution" that turns words into deeds, sentiments into commitments, and complacencies into crusades.

Had not the Philippians seen just this in Paul, their beloved friend and mentor? Had he not shown them, thanks to Christ's grace, what it is to take the "true," the "honourable," the "just," the "pure," the "lovely," the "gracious," and weave them into a pattern of excellence? Not philosophical abstractions but flesh-and-blood demonstrations—these formed the personalized pattern of behaviour set before these Philippian friends to inspire them.

But the adequacy of this inspiration is now enhanced by a further fact, the fact, namely, of God's *peace-giving presence*. "And the God of peace will be with you," is the serenely splendid conclusion of the 9th verse and of the first section of this 4th chapter.

In verse 7 we had "the peace of God" for our *guarding*; here we have "the God of peace" for our *going*. And the second is even greater than the first.

"The God of peace will be with you"—to give you a *humble spirit*. For be well assured that it is pride, with its touchiness and vulnerability to woundings of the ego, that accounts for much of the heart's sourness and restlessness.

"The God of peace will be with you"—to give you *singleness of purpose*. For be well assured that "the double-minded man" is perilously unstable. The heart where divisions has its home is the heart where disquiet has its habitat.

"The God of peace will be with you"—to give you an *ample trust.* For be well assured that somewhere near the core of the soul's unrest is the soul's unbelief. Dr. Walter Cavert tells of a physician of wide experience who analysed the "worriers" who at one time or another had been his patients. Forty per cent of them, he found, worried over things that never happened. Thirty per cent of the worries analysed were related to past matters which were now beyond the patients' control. Twelve per cent were anxious about their health, although their only illness was in their imagination. Ten per cent worried over their families, their friends, or the neighbours, although in most cases there was no substantial basis for the fears that were causing trouble. Just eight per cent of the worries seemed to have some basis in conditions that needed to be remedied.

If this analysis provides us with any approximate gauge of affairs, nine-tenths of our frets are quite needless and useless. It might be added that, from the Christian point of view, the remaining tenth, if surrendered to God, could be handled constructively and the corrosive effect of the fretting effectively counteracted.

Someone to me unknown has written:

"I cannot know why suddenly the storm
Should rage so fiercely round me in its wrath;
But this I know—God watches all my path,
And I can trust.

I may not draw aside the mystic veil
That hides the unknown future from my sight,
Nor know if for me waits the dark or light;
But I can trust.

I have no power to look across the tide,
To see while here the land beyond the river;
But this I know—I shall be God's forever;
So I can trust."

We have been examining the adequacy that belongs to the Christian, as Paul teaches it to his fellow-disciples at Philippi. It is a wide and wealthy and wonderful thing. It includes an adequacy of *love,* of *joy,* of *gentleness,* of *security,* and of *inspiration.*

It remains now for us to determine whether the apostle's own experience will support and seal the teaching that he confidently offers to others.

II

THE ADEQUACY EMPHASIZED IN PAUL'S TESTIMONY

"I rejoice in the Lord greatly that now at length you have revived your concern for me; you were indeed concerned for me, but you had no opportunity. Not that I complain of want; for I have learned, in whatever state I am, to be content. I know how to be abased, and I know how to abound; in any and all circumstances I have learned the secret of facing plenty and hunger, abundance and want. I can do all things in him who strengthens me.

"Yet it was kind of you to share my trouble. And you Philippians yourselves know that in the beginning of the gospel, when I left Macedonia, no church entered into partnership with me in giving and receiving except you only; for even in Thessalonica you sent me help once and again. Not that I seek the gift; but I seek the fruit which increases to your credit. I have received full payment, and more; I am filled, having received from Epaphroditus the gifts you sent, a fragrant offering, a sacrifice acceptable and pleasing to God. And my God will supply every need of yours according to his riches in glory in Christ Jesus" (4: 10–19).

We discover, to begin with, that Paul testified to an adequacy that *masters the extremes of life.* This witness, it is only fair to say, emerges as a by-product of the purpose that lies back of this concluding section of his letter. This purpose is to take the topic of thankfulness to which he made brief allusion in chapter 1, verse 5, and expand it into a full-scale acknowledgment of the timely gift that had come to him by Epaphroditus from the congregation at Philippi. One wonders if there was ever a friend who took more delicate pains with his "thank you" than Paul takes here. He even makes it an occasion to indulge in gentle pleasantries and word-plays. All in all, his message of gratitude justifies Erdman's tribute in calling it "a rare blending of affection, of dignity, of delicacy, with a certain undertone of . . . pleasantry."[1]

[1] C. R. Erdman, *Epistle Of Paul To The Philippians.* Philadelphia: Westminster, p. 131.

It should be pointed out that the extreme care and courtesy with which this section is written are far more vividly and lucidly expressed in later translations than in the Authorized Version. There is clear gain in consulting such translations as those of the Berkeley Version, Weymouth, Phillips, and Williams, along with the Revised Standard Version that we are using.

After expressing his grateful gladness that in sending the gift by Epaphroditus they had found opportunity to be helpful to him again—a helpfulness they would have displayed sooner if they had been given the opportunity—Paul then declares, feelingly, "Not that I complain of want; for I have learned, in whatever state I am, to be content" (v. 11).

Whether the learning process be long or short, to arrive at this goal of healthy contentedness is a boon which, possessed by the masses of men, would turn our society into something approximating Paradise. As things are, the amount of sheer emotional wretchedness, plus the less obsessive shades of discontent, is appalling. In no other way can we account for the fantastic consumption of "tranquillizers" and "sleeping pills" that give drug manufacturers big profits and doctors big problems.

What is lacking is the sort of illumination that had come to Paul, which he likens to an initiation. Borrowing the language of the "mystery cults" of his day, the apostle tells us in verse 12, "I have learned the secret," or, more literally, "I have been initiated." In a moment we shall look at the secret itself, but, meanwhile, see what it does for this man who triumphantly possesses it. It enables him to say: "I know how to be abased, and I know how to abound; in any and all circumstances I have learned the secret of facing plenty and hunger, abundance and want." Phillips has it: "I know now how to live when things are difficult and I know how to live when things are prosperous."

Thus, you see, Christ's adequate man is given mastery over the extremes of life. The pendulum may swing from one side to the other, but the clock keeps ticking without either hurrying or halting.

Life is an endless series of adjustments. Most of them are minor, undramatic, relatively painless. But not infrequently the top blows off the volcano. Life erupts—either in a fierce rain of trouble or a sudden burst of good fortune. Then the acute question is: can we cope with it? If it be trouble, will it flatten us? If it be fortune, will it spoil us?

Some years ago, it will be remembered, Billy Rose wrote a syndicated newspaper column, in which items of extraordinary human interest would frequently appear. One day he told the story of a group of famous American financiers who, in the early 1920's, had met at the Edgewater Beach Hotel in Chicago. They represented, in personal wealth and financial control, more money than there was in the national treasury. From time to time their names appeared in the press. Their influence was enormous, their "success" fabulous.

Twenty-five years later Billy Rose called the roll of these princes of the financial world. The men, whom he freely named, will be nameless here. One of them, a man who had cornered millions through wheat speculation, had died abroad, insolvent. Another, the president of the nation's largest independent steel company, had died broke. The president of the New York Stock Exchange, another in the group, had been recently released from prison. A member of the cabinet in the Harding administration, after being let out of prison for health reasons, had died at home. The greatest exploiter of the "bear" market in Wall Street had committed suicide. The leader of the world's greatest monopoly —that of matches—had likewise died at his own hand. Billy Rose's summing up was sound. He said, "All of these men had learned how to make big money, but not one of them had learned how to live!"

What *they* had "learned" and what *Paul* had "learned" came to them in two totally different schools. Both schools are still running! Both have their enrollees!

As for the "secret" itself, let us exercise care lest we miss it. Some have thought that the secret of contentment is to denounce wealth and to espouse poverty. Paul does neither. He wastes no emotional fury in pronouncing a curse on riches. Nor does he exalt poverty as the ideal state.

The Pauline secret lies in a Christian balance between an outer *attachment* to material concerns and an inner *detachment* from them. Christ's masterful man knows that food and drink, housing and clothing, are necessary to the ongoing of our physical existence and that, beyond the point of minimum necessity, they are desirable, while still falling short of what is extravagant or wasteful; but he knows, also, that his real life does not consist of these material facilities, no, not even of those that may be called necessities.

Somewhere I have read that Socrates was wont to poke around among the market stalls and bazaars of Athens, asking one and another whom he met, "Can you tell me where those things can be bought that are *really* necessary to life?"

And you will remember that in one among many of Thomas Carlyle's outbursts of violent rhetoric in his *Sartor Resartus,* he thunders his query, "Will the whole Finance Ministers and Upholsterers and Confectioners of modern Europe undertake, in joint-stock company, to make one Shoeblack happy?"[1] The point that the volcanic Scot is making is sound beyond debate: it is that man, however lost and sunken, has the dimension of the Infinite in him (God put it there!), an Infinite which, with all man's "cunning, he cannot quite bury under the Finite."

On the other hand, when man is no longer merely God-haunted but is, through Christ, God-happy, it does not matter, in the final resort, whether the "Upholsterers" and the "Confectioners" are many or few: there is God, there is God's Christ; and so the soul, greatly trusting, can never be greatly deprived.

Since the year 1925, when I visited Palestine, I have carried as one of my most vivid memories of that memorable trip the story of the well-known hymn "It Is Well With My Soul," as told to me by the daughter of the author. For all the years of this century and more, Mrs. Bertha Spafford Vester has been identified with the "American Colony" in Jerusalem. She told us about her father, a successful lawyer in Chicago, who was a warm friend of Dwight L. Moody. After the great Chicago fire of 1871 Mr. Spafford made arrangements for the family to have a trip to Europe, Mrs. Spafford and the four daughters to go on ahead, and Mr. Spafford to join them a little later.

The ship on which the happy mother and the happy children sailed, the *Ville du Havre,* never got farther than half-way across the Atlantic. In the "dead" of a November night it was rammed by a sailing vessel and cut in two. In the appalling confusion and disaster that followed Mrs. Spafford saw all four of her girls swept away to their death. A falling mast knocked her unconscious, and a wave freakishly deposited her body on a substantial piece of wreckage where, later, she regained consciousness.

When she and a few other survivors reached Cardiff, Wales, Mrs. Spafford cabled two words to her husband: "Saved alone."[2] Taking the earliest ship he could get, he hastened to Mrs. Spafford's side, all the ache of his heart going out to her and going up to the Father-God. It was when his ship reached the approximate spot where the *Ville du Havre* had met its doom that God gave him the inspiration, the insight, and the courage to write:

[1] T. Carlyle, *Sartor Resartus.* Chicago: McClurg and Co., p. 189.
[2] Mrs. Vester was born later.

"When peace like a river attendeth my way,
When sorrows like sea-billows roll,
Whatever my lot, Thou hast taught me to say:
'It is well, it is well with my soul.'"

Mark those words: "Whatever my lot!" St. Paul would have revelled in them. This is precisely the point of his testimony: "in any and all circumstances I have learned the secret of facing plenty and hunger, abundance and want" (v. 12). We shall be the poorer for it if we miss this mastery over the extremes of life.

Omitting for the moment any reference to verse 13, there is a further aspect of this victorious sufficiency Paul has found in Christ: it is an adequacy that is normally *mediated* through the helpfulness of others. "It was kind of you to share my trouble," Paul writes. Nor was this any new and unexpected gesture of graciousness on their part. He reminds them that "in the beginning of the gospel, when I left Macedonia, no church entered into partnership with me in giving and receiving except you only" (v. 15).

Not all of Paul's greatness is to be seen in his untiring helpfulness *toward* others. Part of it lies in his humble willingness to be helped *by* others. Someone has drawn attention to the three stages of man's growth: (1) dependence (the helpless baby), (2) independence (the cocky adolescent) and (3) inter-dependence (the mature adult).

Is there not a parallel in the growth of the Christian soul? This prince of apostles did not regard his ability, under God, to cope with life in all of its tough and tender phases as a thing apart from the aid of other Christians. It was through them that, in the nick of time, the welcome surcease arrived.

According to the Book of Acts, Jesus once said, "It is more blessed to give than to receive" (Acts 20: 35). True, this puts the *giver* in an elevated place. At the same time we must not *misread* our Lord. No hint did He give that it is not "blessed" to "receive." Indeed, an excellent case can be made for the point that no friendship has progressed very far, nor will it endure at length, unless there is a winsome (though never presumptuous) receptiveness to match a winsome (though never condescending) "givingness." In both roles the artistry of Paul's heart was superb.

"O ray of light, my friend!
When sorrow's gloom made life so drear,
Then comfort sweet thy words did lend
As if Christ spake, 'Be of good cheer.'

O rock of strength, my friend!
When shifting sands beneath my feet,
And changing scenes my steps attend,
Thy truth and constancy are sweet.

I clasp thy hand, my friend!
Thank God that thou art here;
I am not worthy He should send
To me a gift so dear."[1]

See now how the delicacy of this man's soul inscribes its exquisite tracery on the thankfulness he is expressing. It seems suddenly to occur to him that the friends in Philippi might interpret his words concerning that long and repeatedly proven mood of generosity as a bid for yet another gift. Hence the quick assurance: "Not that I seek the gift; but I seek the fruit which increases to your credit" (v. 17).

Since the word rendered "fruit" was a familiar one in the vocabulary of business, being commonly applied to what we should call "interest," it is fair to paraphrase Paul's words: "I do not want the capital but the interest; and it accrues to your account, not mine." Thus tactfully and truthfully are these stewards of the Lord in this beloved congregation reminded that from every generous offering the giver gathers more than the receiver.

Frank P. Fletcher has struck the right note:

"I shared a pilgrim's heavy load:
He shared with me his own.
But each one found, as we trudged on,
His burden lighter grown.

I kept a gladness to myself:
It sickly grew and died.
But when my friend rejoiced with me,
That joy was multiplied.

Who runs may read this law of God
Emblazoned everywhere:
He who would live life at its best
Must share, and share, and share."

Continuing with this semi-commercial manner of speech, the smiling soul of the apostle may be thought of as reaching for a

[1] Quoted by H. D. McKeehan in *Life's Golden Hours*. New York: Revell, pp. 66, 67.

receipt book and filling out the form with a zestful flourish: "I have received full payment, and more; I am filled, having received from Epaphroditus the gift you sent." And then, in a curious blending of the commercial and the sacramental, he describes their gift as "a fragrant offering, a sacrifice acceptable and pleasing to God" (v. 18). Their gift had been made to Paul but, as he now viewed it, it was made supremely to the Lord. That made it a sacrifice. That gave it its aroma of pure love.

Andrew Fuller, a contemporary of William Carey, helped launch the modern movement of foreign missions on its way. It is said that one day he asked for a gift for missions from a friend in the community. Said his friend, "Well, Andrew, I'll give five pounds, seeing it is you." "No," said Fuller, "I can't take anything for this cause, seeing that it is for me you are doing it." Feeling rebuked, the man hesitated a moment, then said, "Andrew, you are right, here are ten pounds seeing it is for the Lord Jesus Christ!" If we give as an accommodation to men, there is flatness in the act; if we give as a dedication to Christ, there is fragrance in it.

"Love is the true economist,
Her weights and measures pass in heaven;
What others lavish on the feast
She to the Lord Himself hath given."[1]

We must now consider the final feature of St. Paul's testimony to the adequacy he has experienced in Christ. We have seen it as a kind of overflowing victoriousness that masters the extremes of life and is normally mediated, at the human level, through the helpful agency of others. It remains for us to look at it as an adequacy that is *measured* by the resources of God in His Son.

We return to verse 13: "I can do all things in him who strengthens me." With this familiarly thrilling sentence we shall associate verse 19: "And my God will supply every need of yours according to his riches in glory in Christ Jesus."

These two verses, though differing in their immediate contexts, both reflect Paul's boundless confidence in the availability of Christ as a living, interior secret of power. "I can do all things *in him.*" "To be 'in Christ'," says Professor James Stewart, "means that Christ is the redeemed man's new environment. The human body, by the acts of eating and drinking and breath-

[1] Quoted by J. G. Mantle in *The Counterfeit Christ.* New York: Revell, p. 111.

ing, is continually drawing for its strength upon the resources of its physical environment. So the Christian spirit, by prayer and worship and surrender, makes contact and keeps contact with its spiritual environment, which is Christ: thus the soul draws for its strength upon the supplies of power which in Christ are quite inexhaustible."[1]

"I can!" How bracing an affirmation this is when it rests in such a faith as Paul is confessing!

It is depressingly easy to find people who know how to say, "I can't." They are well practised in it. You have heard their talk. (Could it be that you have done some of it yourself?) "I can't control my temper." "I can't cope with these jealous thoughts." "I can't stand my mother-in-law." "I can't tithe my income for the Kingdom of God." "I can't take a Sunday School class." "I can't pray in public." "I can't concentrate on my work." "I can't live the holy life I read about in the Scriptures." "I can't be a victorious Christian."

The list is almost endless. The refrain is at times monotonous. "I can't! I can't! I can't!"

Now the way out of this impotence is not to blow on one's hands and try a little harder. That is futile. The ability to cope with ourselves, the world around us, the temptations that environ us, the weaknesses that reside deeply within us—this is not in ourselves.

Adequacy comes through attaching ourselves to the Adequate One. It comes through practising the confidence that whatever Jesus Christ once was, in the days of His visible life on earth, conquering the "powers of darkness" whenever He clashed with them, *He still is,* as availably alive and as vitally available as when He stilled a Galilean tempest or turned the black bereavement of Mary and Martha into a song of hope to celebrate the defeat of death.

Here is something glorious for re-proclamation to the Church of today. The melancholy note of the Christian's ineradicable sinfulness and incessant defeat, with no ray of hope save the endlessly repeated forgiveness of God, has had a strong reassertion with the rise and far-reaching influence of neo-orthodoxy. Once more we need the trumpet-music of Paul. Of course we are all caught, with him, in the fierce strain of the moral struggle. Of course the sharpness, the cunningness, and the persistency of temptation are at times a veritable torture. It was the Paul who knew all

[1] J. S. Stewart, *A Man In Christ*. London: Hodder & Stoughton, pp. 197, 198.

this, tasted all this, battled all this, who nevertheless shouted from the top of the battle-heap, "Thanks be unto God, which always causeth us to triumph in Christ!" (2 Corinthians 2: 14).

How can any one miss it? The adequate man, every bit as unworthy the last day of his life as on the first day of his conversion, is nevertheless not agloom with sin's bondage and bitterness but aglow with Christ's mercy and masterfulness.

Then, turning from purely personal witness to a sure promise and prophecy concerning the Philippians, Paul writes: "And my God will supply every need of yours according to his riches in glory in Christ Jesus" (v. 19).

You have supplied my need, or, at any rate, God has through you. Now, I am confident, He is going to supply your need. He will do it in the exercise of an ability which so far surpasses our own that it can only be described as "his riches in glory." Paul's fondness for this word "riches" is well known. When you think of God, he tells the Romans, you should think of the "riches of his goodness" (2: 4) and the "riches of his wisdom" (11: 33). He writes to the Ephesians about the "riches of his grace" (1: 7) and the "riches of his glory" (1: 18).

In fairness let it be said that some reputable expositors, taking the phrase "riches in glory" in the passage before us as a promise of future reward, would have Paul say, in effect: 'You, my brothers and sisters, have met my need. Let me assure you that God will richly make it up to you at the coming of our Lord, when He will give you your place with Him in glory.'

The better known interpretation is the one that I here adopt. Not future reward but present realization seems clearly to be in the apostle's view as he writes thus.

Consider:

"My God"—how *personal*!

'He is the God, brothers, in whom I have found this secret of contentment of which I have been telling you. God of my fathers? Yes. God and Father of our Lord Jesus Christ? Yes. But what I am now writing to you reflects the inconceivably intimate fact that He is *my* God.'

"Will supply"—how *positive*!

Literally, "will fill up" or "fill to the full."

"Every need of yours"—how *provident*!

A word of caution is due here, but it can wait until we have feasted on the vista of God's supplies to which the apostle points. From the cradle to the grave you and I are simply bundles of *needs*. As the layers of life are peeled off, each fresh unwrapping does but bring to light new needs. When infancy's needs are outgrown, those of childhood follow; these in turn are succeeded by the clamant needs of adolescence. On it goes. Some needs indeed—love, for example—are continuous from birth to death. What a blushing pity it is, therefore, that throngs of human beings, at first too sure of themselves and later so disillusioned as to be cynical, go through this world with no grip upon the tremendous fact that a providing God would love to take them into partnership with Himself, with a flat guarantee that they would never be insolvent again!

But now, the word of caution must be spoken. It is this: full many a time the child of the Father will be called upon to leave the interpretation of "need" in higher hands than his own. No set of Christians since St. Paul's day find it so easy to erect their *wants* into *needs* and their *desires* into *necessities* as the Christians of the Anglo-Saxon world in this twentieth century.

A few years ago one of our sociologists reported the results of a test, in which it was claimed that at the beginning of this century the average American wanted 72 different things and considered 18 of them important. A half-century later Mr. Average American, it is reported, has 496 wants and regards 96 of them as necessary to his happiness. Even "the people of God" are not immune to the effects of the subtle social psychology by which they develop soft notions of what is required in this great business of living.

The spiritual effect can be bad. When our wants, yes, even our whims, are not met, we begin to wonder if Philippians 4: 19 is dependable after all. A sentence from Alexander Maclaren needs to be cut and framed for many of us: "The axiom of Christian faith is that whatever we do not obtain we do not require."

To illustrate: was it in fact a need of St. Paul's to have his "thorn in the flesh" removed? That it was a *desire* is beyond question. But need? No! The need, as God interpreted it, was not for the removal of the thorn but for the reinforcement of the thorn-bearer. That need was met.

Or again: what precisely was Paul's own relation to the truth of verse 19 during the long interval that he was waiting for aid from Philippi? On the shallow, short-term view of life's affairs that some Christians have, the apostle could have begun a complaint. 'Why,' he could have asked, 'why doesn't God supply this need of mine?' Granted, that the need did exist in some measure, it is the sound position of an enlightened faith that when that need reaches the point of crucial urgency, God will meet it. From God's point of view Paul's real need, during those long days of waiting, was the mastery of this lesson of taking life's extremes in stride. That need was met, and met magnificently.

"According to his riches in glory"—what *plenitude*!

This flashing phrase opens up the exhaustless treasures of the divine life and love and the "exceeding great and precious promises" that assure us of their availability. Perhaps we are entitled to press the significance of the words *"according to."* It is not said that He will supply our need *out of* but *according to* His "riches in glory." If a millionaire and I are going down the street together and, being appealed to by a beggar, each of us gives him a shilling, it may be said that both of us gave to him *out of* our resources, but emphatically it cannot be said that my millionaire friend gave to him *according to* his resources. If I gave him a shilling, then relatively my companion should have given him a much bigger sum.

The One whom Paul calls "my God" is no parsimonious dole-dispenser. The Father's infinite capacity for giving is the guarantee of His child's adequacy for living.

> *"All of the joy in a wild bird's nest,*
> *All that God hid in a violet's breast,*
> *All the soft wonder of twilight and star,*
> *All that white caravans bring from afar,*
> *All the wealth brought to earth from heaven above—*
> *All are yours as the gift of Christ's love."*[1]

"In Christ Jesus"—what *presence*!

Maclaren has a comment here so picturesque and pithy that I must share it:

> "When Paul says 'riches in glory,' he puts them up high above our reach, but when he adds 'in Christ Jesus,' he brings them all down amongst us. In Him is 'infinite riches in a narrow room.' If we are in Him, then we are beside our treasure, and have only to put out our hands and take the wealth that is lying there. All that we need is 'in Christ,' and if we are in Christ it is all close at our sides."[2]

[1] Quoted by F. Shannon in *The New Personality*. New York: Revell, p. 166.

[2] A. Maclaren, *Expositions of Holy Scripture,* Vol. XIV. Grand Rapids: Eerdmans, p. 73.

The testimony of God's adequate man is in! The record stands. To these Philippians, who know him so well, he has borne witness to an adequacy that masters the extremes of human experience, that is mediated through the helpfulness of God-guided friends, and that is measured by nothing short of the resources of God in His Son.

The effect of all this is to take the *cannot* out of life and put *can* in its place. It looses us from impotence and links us with omnipotence. If a graphic summing up is needed, it might be built around the little word "all" (following the Authorized Version) in verses 12, 13, and 19.

First, there is the "all" of circumstances to be borne; but Paul is adequate: God has given him *poise*.

Second, there is the "all" of things to be done; but Paul is adequate: God has given him *power*.

Third, there is the "all" of needs to be met; but Paul is adequate: God has given him *plenty*.

It is enough—and more!

III

CONCLUSION

"To our God and Father be glory for ever and ever. Amen.

"Greet every saint in Christ Jesus. The brethren who are with me greet you. All the saints greet you, especially those of Caesar's household.

"The grace of the Lord Jesus Christ be with your spirit" (4: 20–23).

There remains to be discharged a threefold courtesy:

1. *A doxology.* Evening is descending on the Imperial City. Tomorrow morning Epaphroditus is leaving Rome for Philippi. He will carry with him the letter that Paul has been dictating. The amanuensis has been recording thoughts and emotions which, without his having any dream of it, will live long after the palace of Caesar has been pulverized. And now the greatest of humans reaches over and, taking the stylus from his secretary's hand, writes out in big, uneven script: "To our God and Father be glory for ever and ever. Amen."

"Glory" here is not the same as in the preceding verse, even though the one may have suggested the other. Here the "glory" is *praise.* God has used the Philippians to supply Paul's need.

Paul is sure that somehow God will supply their need. What, then, more natural than for *both* to unite in adoring thankfulness rendered to Him "from whom all blessings flow." Moreover, since praise is the perpetual pulse of the Christian soul and the Christian Church, what is *now* given to God flows into a stream of adoration that goes on "for ever and ever."

2. *A salutation.* Is it the greeting that is to be "in Christ Jesus" or is it the saint who is "in Christ Jesus"? The Greek scholars tell us that we can have it either way. The grammatical construction is not decisive. Our chief interest should be in the remarkable fact that no "saint," however slow, or dull, or carnal, or difficult, is to go without a greeting.

The circle of greetings and of greeters enlarges: "The brethren who are with me greet you." Who were they? One expositor remarks that it is "surprising and disappointing" that in a letter as informal and intimate as this the apostle failed to be more specific about his companions.[1] One reasonably presumes that the friends in question were those who, from other sources, are known to have visited Paul during his Roman imprisonment: Tychicus, Timothy, Aristarchus, Mark, Luke, and others.

"The brethren who are with me!" The words set some exciting thoughts in motion. Think of the honour that was theirs in being associated with St. Paul. Could they possibly have known how much they were to be envied? Did they feel toward the apostle, I wonder, as Sir Robert Stopford declared Lord Nelson's men felt about him? Stopford was one of Nelson's junior officers. He commanded one of the Admiral's ships on a long sea chase against the enemy, which took them far over to the West Indies. The adventure was one of enormous risk and hardship. Nevertheless, Stopford, in a letter to a friend, wrote: "We are half-starved, and otherwise inconvenienced by being so long out of port. But our reward is—we are with Nelson!" One likes to think that even as the spell of Nelson's naval genius was upon his men, so the spell of Paul's spiritual greatness lay over these companions of his. Always it is a glorious thing to be in close company with those who, handsomely unaware of it themselves, are the intimates of the King!

The circle expands again: "All the saints greet you, especially those of Caesar's household." Thorough research by such scholars as Lightfoot have shown convincingly that this is a reference not to members of the royal family but to some of the

[1] Cf. C. E. Simcox, *They Met At Philippi*. New York: Oxford University Press, p. 157.

domestic and civil servants who were required to maintain the palace.

Lotus flowers lift their pure faces to the sun from settings that are dismal and foul. There were Christians in Paul's day who lived in the moral victory of Christ amid surroundings that were incredibly sensual and difficult. It can be done!

Who were these? We do not know. We need not. It is sufficient that God knows.

"One feast, of holy days the crest,
I, though no Churchman, love to keep,
All-Saints,—the unknown good that rest
In God's still memory folded deep;
The bravely dumb that did their deed,
And scorned to blot it with a name,
Men of the plain heroic breed,
That loved Heaven's silence more than fame.

Such lived not in the past alone,
But thread to-day the unheeding street,
And stairs to Sin and Famine known
Sing with the welcome of their feet;
The den they enter grows a shrine,
The grimy sash an oriel burns,
Their cup of water warms like wine,
Their speech is filled from Heavenly urns.

About their brows to me appears
An aureole traced in tenderest light,
The rainbow-gleam of smiles through tears
In dying eyes, by them made bright,
Of souls that shivered on the edge
Of that chill ford repassed no more,
And in their mercy felt the pledge
And sweetness of the farther shore."[1]

3. *The benediction.* When St. Paul wrote his letters, he concluded with something fairer and finer than the customary "Farewell." The briefest of his benedictions comes at the end of the Colossian epistle: "Grace be with you." The longest comes at the close of 2 Corinthians: "The grace of the Lord Jesus Christ

[1] James Russell Lowell, used by Frederick F. Shannon in *The Infinite Artist.* New York: The Macmillan Company, p. 22.

and the love of God and the fellowship of the Holy Spirit be with you all."

The benediction pronounced on the Philippians is of medium length: "The grace of the Lord Jesus Christ be with your spirit."

But whether long or short, no benediction of Paul's is complete without "grace." The wheel has made a full turn: the apostle having begun with grace (1 : 2), ends with grace. "Grace is more than pardon," writes Professor Moffatt, "it is power, the divine power which redeems life and also uses it, rendering a man efficient for service." Later, he adds: "When the heart of Christian faith comes to the lips, as in some of the classical prayers and hymns, it is—

'Plenteous grace with Thee is found,
grace to cover all my sin;
Let the healing streams abound,
make and keep me pure within.'

The sinful heart requires to be kept no less than made clean."[1]

This insight of Moffatt's is sound. Grace is the pardoning, purifying, beautifying activity of God—all forever undeserved—making something winsomely useful and redemptively charming out of a Saul of Tarsus, or a hot-tempered Peter, or a faint-hearted Timothy, or one of these moral lepers who were attached to Nero's palace.

The final phrase, "with your spirit" (which represents the wording of the best manuscripts), has one detail worthy of notice. "Spirit" appears in the singular, when we might have expected it in the pural. In the plural it would signify that innermost, topmost, bottommost capacity of man for communion with God. It is here that man is crucially dead to God until quickened and changed by the ministry of the Holy Spirit.

"Spirit" in the singular, however, suggests that Paul has in mind the inner life of these Christians as viewed *collectively, corporately*. Does not a congregation have a spirit, which may be a distinctive dullness on the one hand or a distinctive alertness on the other? It may be a spirit of dissension or a spirit of love and of love's deep harmony. Seeing, as we have, the threatened "breach of the peace" in the life of the Philippian church, it may well be that Paul's "singular" here is of set purpose. It says,

[1] Moffatt, *Grace In The New Testament*. New York: Ray Long and Richard Smith, pp. 226, 237.

in effect, 'Brothers, recall what I have already told you in this letter. I told you to treat one another with the same spirit as you experience in Christ Jesus.[1] I told you what that spirit was—the spirit of humble unselfishness that led Christ in grace to empty Himself and become a "servant." This, in turn, led to His being exalted as Lord, a fact that has made you what you are, and all other Christians as well, namely, a fellowship of God. I told you that, as he "never thought of Himself, neither must you think of yourselves first and foremost."'

This is the grace, this indeed is the resultant graciousness, that the affectionate apostle invokes upon these beloved friends of his at Philippi.

The greatest of humans has written his warmest of letters. The love-task is finished. The day is done. The chain is still there upon the apostolic wrist. The soldier is still on guard. Never mind! Paul's spirit is free! His mind is clear! His heart is glowing!

And next morning Epaphroditus strides away to Philippi!

[1] Cf. Moffatt translation of 2: 5.